UN

Th
th
Fა
bc

LITERARY SOURCES
OF SECULAR MUSIC
IN ITALY (CA. 1500)

Da Capo Press Music Reprint Series

GENERAL EDITOR

FREDERICK FREEDMAN

VASSAR COLLEGE

LITERARY SOURCES OF SECULAR MUSIC IN ITALY (CA. 1500)

By Walter H. Rubsamen

DA CAPO PRESS • NEW YORK • 1972

Library of Congress Cataloging in Publication Data

Rubsamen, Walter Howard, 1911-
    Literary sources of secular music in Italy (ca. 1500).

    (Da Capo Press music reprint series)
    Reprint of the 1943 ed., which was issued as v. 1,
no. 1, of University of California publications in
music.
    "Appendix of musical examples": p.
    Bibliography: p.
    1. Music and literature. 2. Italian poetry—16th
century—History and criticism. 3. Songs, Italian—
History and criticism. 4. Part-songs, Italian—To 1800.
I. Title. II. Series: California. University.
University of California publications in music, v. 1,
no. 1.
ML180.R8   1972   780'.08   72-4482
ISBN 0-306-70496-X

This Da Capo Press edition of *Literary Sources of Secular Music in Italy (ca. 1500)* is an unabridged republication of the first edition published in Berkeley and Los Angeles in 1943 as Volume 1, Number 1 (Pages 1-82) of the *University of California Publications in Music*. It is reprinted by special arrangement with the author.

Published by Da Capo Press, Inc.
A Subsidiary of Plenum Publishing Corporation
227 West 17th Street, New York, New York 10011

LITERARY SOURCES OF SECULAR MUSIC IN ITALY (CA. 1500)

Strambotti by Serafino Aquilano in the Biblioteca Trivulziana, Milan, MS 55.

LITERARY SOURCES OF SECULAR MUSIC IN ITALY (CA. 1500)

BY

WALTER H. RUBSAMEN

UNIVERSITY OF CALIFORNIA PRESS

BERKELEY AND LOS ANGELES

1943

University of California Publications in Music
Editors (Los Angeles): G. S. McManus, W. H. Rubsamen
Volume 1, No. 1, pp. 1–82, frontispiece
Submitted by editors April 4, 1941
Issued March 20, 1943
Price, $1.25

University of California Press
Berkeley, California

————

Cambridge University Press
London, England

CONTENTS

I. FORM AND CONTENT OF THE FROTTOLA: A GENERAL BACKGROUND

THE SAYING, "Music is a handmaiden of poetry," may be applied most appropriately to the secular vocal music of the Italian Renaissance, including the period under discussion here (*ca.* 1470 to *ca.* 1520), since much of the verse then in vogue was believed suitable for recitation only when wedded to the tonal art. Yet the two components of this synthesis were hardly of equal importance to the contemporary audience. Poetry seems always to have been the starting point in a creative process, whereas music was added merely as a means of heightening the general effect.

Characteristics of musical style in the *frottola*, the categorical name for tonal settings of secular poetry in this period, have been analyzed at length[1] and will therefore be mentioned here but briefly. The role of secular music as a vehicle for the lyricism of Italian poets and as a means of courtly entertainment has, on the other hand, received less attention. The texts of the *frottole*, once of primary interest, have remained too long under a shroud of anonymity. Since many of Italy's foremost poets contributed to this literature, it seems of value to establish wherever possible their authorship of verse in musical setting and to describe the circumstances which gave rise to such a union of the arts. Much has been written concerning the political and literary activities of Lorenzo de' Medici, the sculpture and painting of Michelangelo, the humanism of Sannazzaro and Bembo, and the courtly philosophy of Castiglione, but little has been said of their share in the development of secular music or of the part it played in their lives. To shed more light upon the manner in which their verses and those of other noteworthy contemporaries were embellished with lyrical accompaniments is the purpose of this investigation.

During the *quattrocento* countless amateurs who used Petrarca's amorous lyricism as a model had found that Italian was an ideal language for versification. Courtiers and members of the populace alike were able to express their emotions in a language seemingly built for rhyming. Their poems, passed from mouth to mouth, were often awkward and absurdly sentimental, yet possessed so fundamental an appeal that cultivated men of letters also strove to infuse into their writings some of the vigor of plebeian verse. Thus, professional poets imitated the content as well as the form of the most popular verse schemes, the *strambotto* (or *rispetto*) and the *barzelletta-frottola*. The *strambotto,* probably of Sicilian origin, was a pet medium for passionate outbursts of all kinds, including the wails of jilted lovers or of the unhappily married, as well as the brazen confessions of girls eager for romance.

One of the first poets of talent to favor the *strambotto* as a vehicle for the expression of pseudo-proletarian emotions was the Venetian, Leonardo Giusti-

---

[1] Rudolf Schwartz, "Die Frottole im 15. Jahrhundert," *Vierteljahrsschrift für Musikwissenschaft*, II (1886), 427 ff.; *idem, Ottaviano Petrucci, Frottole, Buch I und IV,* Publikationen älterer Musik . . . der Deutschen Gesellschaft für Musikwissenschaft, VIII (Leipzig, Br. u. H., 1933–1935), Einleitung; Knud Jeppesen, *Die mehrstimmige italienische Laude um 1500* (Leipzig: Br. u. H., 1935), Einleitung.

niani (1388–1446). His verses seem often to have been garnished with musical accompaniments and to have gained much from the addition. The tenderly simple *O Rosa bella,* best known in Dunstable's setting,[2] was a favorite lyric for composers of the middle *quattrocento.* Giustiniani himself wrote music to a great many of his amorous lyrics, which seem to have been esteemed by the contemporary public just as much for the manner in which they were performed as for their literary merit. Throughout the sixteenth century the name *Justiniana* continued to be associated with a species of light, entertaining vocal music, the texts of which had little in common with Leonardo's own verses. By this time, of course, many musicians were no longer aware that the form had originally been named after a poet. Thomas Morley, in his *A plaine and easie introduction to practicall musicke,*[3] indulges in a ridiculous speculation which he believes will satisfactorily explain the genesis of the *Justiniana:* "There is likewise a kind of songs . . . called Justinianas, and are all written in the Bergamasca language : a wanton and rude kind of musicke it is, and like enough to carrie the name of some notable Curtisan of the Citie of Bergama, for no man will deny that Justiniana is the name of a woman." [!] Dr. Alfred Einstein, having transcribed all available examples of the form, concludes that the *Justiniana* of the later sixteenth century was created by Andrea Gabrieli and his circle. It is always three-voiced and its music differs not a whit from that of the *villanella alla napoletana.* The sentiments expressed are those of an old, scatterbrained Venetian patrician who stutters in the dialect of Venice, not, as Morley believed, in the Bergamascan, and who seems to have been modeled after a member of the Giustiniani family.

Many poets of the later *quattrocento* were also subject to proletarian influences and responded as had Giustiniani. Lorenzo de' Medici (1449–1492) and Poliziano (1454–1494) are but two of the many literati whose contributions to the *frottola* will be the subject of detailed analysis in the main body of this study.

During the period under discussion, much of the verse heard from the lips of the populace was composed by anonymi of ability far inferior to that of the poets cited. Lyrics in the democratic vein by cultivated artists were often exquisitely beautiful, but the greater part of those set to music were commonplace and derivative, originating in the streets. Stemming from the pens of humble and ignorant rhymsters, such verse must nevertheless not be confused with folk song, since most of it is thoroughly impregnated with pseudo-aristocratic sentimentality. Most of the *frottola* literature, then, was composed by amateurs who usually relied upon a patchwork of phrases borrowed from others. Their models were the *strambotti* and *barzellette* of talented professional poets who had at first been inspired by the popular muse, but who now poured the artistry of an intellectual aristocracy into simple molds of humble origin. Pseudo-plebeian verse by men of recognized literary standing was

---

[2] A. W. Ambros, *Geschichte der Musik* (2d ed.; Leipzig, 1880), II, Musikbeilagen, 22.

[3] Facsimile edition by the Shakespeare Association, No. 14 (London: Oxford Univ. Press, 1937), p. 180.

disseminated throughout Italy, setting the tone for a host of prolific imitators. The passionate *strambotti* of a Pulci or a Serafino prompted romantic dilettantes to utterances which dealt for the most part with love's misery, but which were rarely intended for consumption at face value. How often are sentimentalities expressed with tongue in cheek! How frequently ironical are the amorous heroics, dear to courted hearts!

The flood of verses in this vein is preserved for us in musical setting not only in the eleven books of *frottole* published by Ottaviano Petrucci between the years 1504 and 1514 in Venice and Fossombrone, but also in a great many contemporary manuscripts and prints.[4] From the plenitude of source material I have attempted to segregate and identify works by men of accepted literary rank, whose verses were obviously exemplary to the layman.

The music of Petrucci's *frottole* and that of contemporary collections is in general unsophisticated; most of it was written by composers who were unaware or impatient of polyphonic complexity. In each composition the uppermost voice, sometimes even the entire complex of parts, is intimately related to the text, the length and accent of a musical phrase being subservient to the demands of its verse. The poetical form chosen usually determined the musical pattern. If the initial text of a *barzelletta*, for example, were to be reiterated as a refrain, a composer would quite naturally choose to repeat the opening music, creating a tripartite form (see No. 1 of the Appendix). Such a tonal setting may seem elaborate, but when dissected is found to con-

---

[4] A collation of Schwartz (see note 1 above), Pub. ält. Musik, VIII, v–vii; and Jeppesen, "Ueber einige unbekannte Frottolenhandschriften," *Acta Musicologica*, XI, fasc. 3 (July–Sept., 1939), 112–114, will furnish a list of collections available to musicologists at the present time. The survival in Italy of a probably unique copy of *Frottole intabulate da sonar organi, libro primo. Impresso in Roma per Andrea Anticho da Montona nel anno MCXVII a. di. XVII di gennaro* seems, however, to have escaped the attention of both authors. This work, the first printed example of Italian organ tablature, belongs to the family of the Marchesi Polesini in Parenzo and its contents are analyzed by Anteo Gravisi in *Atti e Memorie della Società Istriana di Archeologia e Storia Patria*, I, fasc. 1–2 (Parenzo, 1885), 143–144. Since the periodical mentioned is usually difficult of access, the *tavola* of Antico's collection is reprinted here: *Amor, quando fioriva mia speme*—B[artolomeo] T[romboncino] [poem by Petrarca]; *Animoso mio desire*—T. B. [B. T.]; *Che farala, che dirala*—B. T. [Don Michele in Petrucci XI, 26, and in Vogel, 1517[1]]; *Che deggio fare?*—B. T. [Petrarca]; *Crudel, fugi se sai!*—M[arco] C[ara; but B.T. in Vogel, 1518[1]] [Galeotto del Carretto]; *Chi non crede che al mondo el sol nutrisca*—B. T.; *Cantai, mentre nel core*—M. C. [Bald. Castiglione; folio missing]; *Dolci ire, dolci sdegni*—B. T. [Petrarca]; *Fiamma amorosa e bella*—B. T. [but M. C. in Vogel, 1518[1]]; *Frena, donna, i tuoi bei lumi*—[anon.]; *Gentil donna, se in voi*—B. T.; *Hor che'l ciel e la terra*—B. T. [Petrarca]; *La non vol esser più mia*—B. T. [Poliziano]; *Me lassaratu mo*—Ranier; *Non più morte al mio morire*—B. T.; *Non resta in questa valle*—[anon.]; *O che aiuto, o che conforto*—[M. C. in Vogel, 1517[1]]; *O che dirala mo*—B. T.; *Ochi mei lassi*—B. T. [Petrarca; B. T. in *Canzoni nove*, 41]; *Odi, ciel, il mio lamento*—B. T.; *Per mio ben te vederei*—B. T.; *Per doler me bagno el viso*—M. C.; *Si è debile il filo*—B. T. [Petrarca]; *Stavasi amor dormendo sotto un fagio*—B. T.; *Son io quel che era quel dì*—B. T.; *Vergine bella*—B. T. [Petrarca]. The sole right to print organ tablatures had been granted to Ottaviano Petrucci by Pope Leo X in 1513, but the famous publisher failed to take advantage of his monopoly and lost it to Antico through a papal breve issued December 27, 1516. See Augusto Vernarecci, *Ottaviano de' Petrucci da Fossombrone* (2d ed.; Bologna, 1882), pp. 141 ff., 177–181. Not knowing exactly what is meant by organ tablature, Vernarecci assumes it to be the same as sacred vocal music, and therefore cannot understand why the Pope writes, referring to Petrucci: "... *quamvis iam per triennium et amplius nihil ejus generis* [tablatures] *edidit, sed nostram et aliorum expectationem frustra suspensam tenuit, harum serie derogamus.* ..."

sist of a few well-defined melodic phrases which have been repeated here and there, forming a basic structure made up of sections and resulting in unusual clarity of form.

Petrucci's collective term, *frottole,* includes many different types of verse, to wit: the *strambotto,* the *barzelletta* or *frottola* itself, the ode, *capitolo,* sonnet, *canzone,* and several others. The generic name *frottola,* which is probably derived from the medieval Latin *frocta,* may be defined as "an assortment or bouquet of enjoyable things" (in this case, verses). More specifically, during the fourteenth and fifteenth centuries the term designated a poem, also called *motti confetti,* of irregular rhyme scheme and length of line containing proverbs or witty sayings. Petrucci, however, as we have seen, uses *frottole* as a convenient title for his conglomeration of many verse schemes, and also for a specific type of poetry in musical setting, the *barzelletta,* which was not at all related to the *frottola* of the *trecento.*

Most of the literature under discussion consists of *barzellette-frottole* and two other proletarian forms which reflect popular tastes and sentiments, the *strambotto* and ode (so-called). These and others of similar character are uniformly regular in rhyme schemes and length of lines, traits which seem to be inherent in verse written by or dedicated to the masses.

The *ballata* of the golden age in Italian literature, of Petrarca, Boccaccio, and Sacchetti, was probably a direct ancestor of the *barzelletta.* Although the *ballata* was superior in literary quality, the two genres are related through the identity of their component parts: *ripresa* and strophe, the strophe being subdivided into *mutazione* and *volta.* However, a Petrarchan *ballata* is irregular in length of line, whereas regularity is an essential feature of the *barzelletta,* the most common pattern of which (in musical setting) comprises a *ripresa* of four trochaic octosyllabic lines (rhyming *abba* or *abab*), followed by a strophe of six or eight similar lines[5] (*mutazione: cdcd; volta: da* or *deea*) and a refrain, the repetition of half or all of the *ripresa.* Both examples printed in the Appendix (Nos. 1 and 2) are of the eight-line variety. More rare are the *frottole* written in iambic septisyllabic lines, with or without refrain. The strophe is then of four lines, rhyming *cddb,* or even *ccca* as in the following composition by P. Zanìn Bisàn:[6]

(*ripresa*)	*O despietato tempo,*	(strophe)	*Dio sa quanto mi doglio*
	Contrario a ogni ben mio!		*De l'aspro tuo cordoglio,*
	Amante, va con dio,		*Ma sappi ch'esser voglio*
	Chè adesso non è tempo.		*Tua serva in ogni tempo.*

There are of course many minor variants of these fundamental schemes to be found in the *barzellette* of Lorenzo de' Medici, Poliziano, Serafino, and others.[7]

---

[5] The meter within a strophe may on occasion change from trochaic to iambic. See F. Flamini, "Francesco Galeota ... e il suo inedito canzoniere," *Giornale Storico della Letteratura Italiana,* XX (1892), 55.

[6] Petrucci, *Frottole, Lib. VII* (1507), fol. 50'; also Vogel, 1509¹, 16, and in Firenze, R. Ist. Mus., MS 2441. For a biography of the composer see G. d'Alessi, "Zanìn Bisàn," *Note d'Archivio,* VIII (Jan., 1931), 21 ff.

[7] See Rodolfo Renier in the Rassegna Bibliografica, *Giorn. Stor.,* IX (1887), 301–302; also G. Manacorda, "Galeotto del Carretto ... ," *Memorie della R. Accad. delle Scienze di Torino,* Ser. II, XLIX, 2 (1900), 108.

The preferable form for an amorous compliment at the turn of the fifteenth century seems to have been the *strambotto,* the pattern of which may be described as a succession of eight-line (iambic endecasyllabic) strophes, in this exceedingly regular rhyme scheme: *abababcc* (see Appendix, No. 3). Under the title of ode Petrucci groups a number of verse schemes, all of which have strophes of four lines in iambic meter. The first three lines are always septisyllabic, whereas the last can be of 4, 5, 7, or even 11 syllables. Middle lines of each strophe rhyme, but the last interlocks with the first of the subsequent strophe, to wit:

abbc cdde ef, etc.   or   *aaab bbbc c,* etc.
7774 7774 77   7774 7774 7
or 11   11
or 7   7

Printed in the Appendix is an example of the former type (No. 4).

How were these poems performed when set to music? In Petrucci's editions and in contemporary manuscripts a complete text usually appears only under the uppermost voice of each composition. This has been accepted as proof that the other parts were intended for instruments, yet there are legitimate reasons to believe that in some compositions all parts were sung in *a cappella* chorus. An anecdote sustaining this contention is related by Captain Galeazzo Visconti in a letter to Isabella d'Este,[8] in which he describes a pleasure trip to the forests of Cusago in the company of Beatrice Sforza, Duchess of Milan, and her court fool Dioda: "This morning, Friday, the duchess, all her gentlewomen, and I mounted horse and rode to Cusago; and in order to advise your excellency of our diversions I shall tell you that at the start of our journey I was required to join the duchess and Dioda in her carriage, where *we sang more than 25 songs, very well harmonized for 3 voices,* that is, *Dioda the tenor, and I sometimes bass and sometimes soprano, and the duchess soprano.* We said and did so many foolish things that I seem now to have gained the distinction of being crazier than Dioda" (italics mine). Secondly, in the frontispiece[9] of the *Canzoni nove,* a collection published in 1510, there are depicted four merry gentlemen *singing* lustily from a single book, seemingly without aid of instruments. We may assume, therefore, that *frottole* were performed in all the different ways mentioned by Baldassare Castiglione in his *Cortegiano,*[10] that is, by an individual who sings to instrumental accompaniment, by several voices singing in chorus, by a player upon a keyboard instrument, or by a string quartet. Some subsidiary parts in *frottole* are unmistakably instrumental in character. Others, however, are melodies which flow quietly within a legitimate vocal range; if in addition the text fits easily, one may assume that such parts are singable.[11] The *a cappella* performance of several of the compositions printed in the Appendix seems feasible, and for these the missing text has been inserted within parentheses.

---

[8] A. Luzio and R. Renier, "Delle relazioni di Isabella d'Este Gonzaga con Ludovico e Beatrice Sforza," *Archivio Storico Lombardo,* Ser. II, VII (1890), 108.

[9] Facsimile in Schwartz, Pub. ält. Musik, VIII (after p. xlv).

[10] *The Book of the Courtier,* trans. by L. E. Opdyke (New York, 1903), pp. 88–89.

[11] See Schwartz, "Nochmals 'Die Frottole im 15. Jahrhundert,'" *Jahrbuch der Musikbibliothek Peters,* XXXI (1924), 57.

Collections of *frottole* compiled before 1510, including Petrucci's first nine volumes, were devoted almost exclusively to the assortment of unsophisticated verses that I have mentioned, that is, the *barzellette-frottole, strambotti,* odes, and the like, but occasional examples of more aristocratic poetry may also be found. Here and there in the mass of mean rhymes there were sonnets and *canzoni,* forms of classical repute because the idolized Petrarca had employed them in his immortal *Canzoniere.* These were considered unquestionably elegant by the rhymsters of *frottole,* as were also the polished verses in *terza rima* called *capitoli,* which were long poems in strophes of three iambic endecasyllabic lines, rhyming *aba bcb cdc,* etc. The final strophe could also be extended to four lines, as in the example printed in the Appendix (No. 5).

As soon as such verses of quality began to displace the others to an appreciable degree, the trend toward a more artistic form of secular vocal music was established. In other words, with the gradual refinement of poetic standards in collections of *frottole* one of the necessary steps in the direction of a more consummate work of art, the madrigal, had been initiated.

If the inclusion of a sonnet or *canzone* in early prints or manuscripts of *frottole* had been of rare occurrence, the exception became a rule in collections compiled during the second and third decades of the *cinquecento.* The new bent may be distinctly recognized with the publication of Andrea Antico's *Canzoni nove* (1510), in which appeared no less than seven of Petrarca's lyrics, a *canzone* by the distinguished humanist Jacopo Sannazzaro, entitled *Valle riposte e sole,* and other verses of high literary value. In Petrucci's eleventh book of *frottole,* published in 1514, poems for the populace were for the first time in the minority, there being only twenty-one *barzellette* and six *strambotti* in comparison with forty-one examples of more literary types: *canzoni,* sonnets, and *capitoli.*[12]

How the change of taste affected patron and composer alike is clearly indicated in a letter[13] which was written in September, 1514, by the famous musician Marco Cara. Having received from the young prince Frederic Gonzaga certain newly composed verses, with the request that he employ all his art in their musical setting, Cara replies that his juvenile patron is justified in being enthusiastic, for the poems really *seem of antique origin,* conceived and formed during the era of the learned Dante and the delectable Petrarca. This statement is an epitome of the newly accepted standard by which musical poetry was henceforth to be judged. It also illuminates the contemporary attitude toward the greatest of Italian poets. Dante was not sufficiently elegant for the courtiers of the period, and his pungent realism often made them uncomfortable. In Petrarca, on the other hand, they found that ideal combination of tender melancholy and restrained passion couched in polished terms which expressed so admirably their own amorous philosophy. Among musicians of the sixteenth century, Petrarca enjoyed by far the greater favor. Most composers of *frottole* and madrigals were required, of course, to comply with the

---

[12] Jeppesen, *Die mehrstimmige italienische Laude,* pp. xxvi–xxvii.
[13] Quoted by A. Luzio, in the Rassegna Bibliografica, *Giorn. Stor.,* XVII (1891), 106.

known preferences of their patrons, and they thus neglected even the lyrical poems by the author of the *Divina commedia*. I can add but a single musical setting of Dante, the *canzone, Amor, da che convien che pur mi doglia*,[14] to that believed unique during the first half of the *cinquecento* (*Così nel mio parlare*).[15]

To identify the examples, at first isolated, of refined verse schemes is of great consequence in tracing the stylistic development from *frottola* to madrigal. Rudolph Schwartz, in his original article on the *frottola*,[16] made a preliminary examination of the source materials then at his disposal, and established the fact that a few classical poems were scattered throughout Petrucci's *Libri I–IX*. Petrarca's sonnet, *Ite, caldi sospiri*, set to music by the Veronese Jo. Brochus, was published in *Lib. III;*[17] several *canzoni* by Petrarca and Bembo in *Lib. VII* (see below, pp. 24–25, 27, and Appendix, Nos. 7–10); Petrarca's sonnet, *O tempo, o ciel volubil*, and *sestina, Mia benigna fortuna*, in *Lib. IX;* Horace's ode, *Integer vitae*, set by the Veronese Don Michael Pesenti in *Lib. I;*[18] and Dido's lament from the *Aeneid* of Vergil, *Dissimulare etiam*, harmonized by Ph. de Lurano in *Lib. VIII*.

It is hardly necessary to stress the superiority of Petrarchan or Latin conception and content over the norm of the *barzelletta* or *strambotto*. Enough evidence may be derived from a comparison of the subject matter and technique in *canzoni* with that in uncultivated verses; examples of both are printed in the Appendix. The growing popularity of the musical *canzone* in particular is an evidence of reaction to the all-too-great formal regularity of popular verse schemes. A strophe of the *canzone* is characterized by free alternation between endeca- and septisyllabic lines, the number of which is optional and the rhyming irregular, except that the last two lines are usually matched. When such a pattern is harmonized, greater rhythmic variety results, since the musical accentuation is no longer bound to the ever-recurring trochaic octosyllabic or iambic endecasyllabic line.

The only difference between the scheme of the classical *canzone* and of the

---

[14] Venice, Bibl. Marciana, MSS Italiani Cl. IV, No. 1795–1798, no. 79 (see Jeppesen, "Ueber einige unbekannte Frottolenhandschriften," *Acta Musicologica*, XI, 98). The poem may be found in Dante Alighieri, *Opere minori* (Firenze, 1861), I, 130.

[15] Alfred Einstein, "Dante, on the Way to the Madrigal," *Musical Quarterly*, XXV, 2 (April, 1939), 144, 155.

[16] "Die Frottole im 15. Jahrhundert," *Viertelj. f. Musikw.*, II (1886), 427 ff.

[17] Reprinted in modern notation by Arnold Schering, *Geschichte der Musik in Beispielen* (Leipzig: Br. u. H., 1931), no. 70.

[18] *Ibid.*, no. 74, in the version for solo voice and lute accompaniment (Vogel, 1509[1]). Other Latin poems set by the frottolists are Michael Pesenti's *In hospitas per alpes*, Petr. *Lib. I*, fol. 53': *Quercus juncta columna est*, to celebrate the wedding of the first Marc' Antonio Colonna to a member of the della Rovere family, in *Lib. IX*, 2; Hie. Alauro's *Laura romanis decorata pompis*, in *Lib. XI*, no. 63; Tromboncino's excerpt from Dido's letter to Aeneas, *Aspicias utinam quae sit scribentis imago*, Ovid, *Her.* VII, 183, which Alfred Einstein transcribed from 1516[1] and published in the *Rassegna Musicale*, X, 2 (Feb., 1937), "La prima 'lettera amorosa' in musica"; Cara's *Quicumque ille fuit puerum*, Propertius, *Eleg.* II, 12, and *Quis furor tanti rabiesque*, see Einstein's ed. of *Canzoni, sonetti ...* , Smith College Music Archives, IV, nos. 21, 22; Vergil's *Dulces exuviae* from the *Aeniad*, IV, 651 in 1519[1]: and Tromboncino's version of Giovanni Pontano's *Cum rides mihi*, in *Frottole de M. Bort. Tromboncino e de M. M. Cara ...* , fol. 20.

form called "madrigal" by musicians (*ca.* 1530) is the occasional symmetry of rhymes or equivalence of syllables in sections of the earlier form. Even this modicum of regularity is lost in most of the newer *canzoni* written during the second and third decades of the *cinquecento,* an illustration being Michelangelo's *Come harò dunque ardire* ... , set to music by Tromboncino and published in 1518.[19] Poetically, even those earlier *canzoni* of Petrucci's *Lib. VII* (1507) are almost identical with the madrigal, yet they are still *frottole* in that they are set strophically, that is, the same music is repeated for each stanza, whereas the music of a madrigal changes constantly in art-song fashion. The musical styles differ in other fundamental respects, but it is evident that the poetical form and content of the madrigal existed some decades prior to its nominal revival as the title of a publication in 1530.[20]

To whom did Petrucci cater when he printed the musical arrangements of elegant and distinctive poetry? Probably to the Italian nobility—patrons of the arts whose good taste is proverbial—to literary-minded poets and musicians, and to an ever-growing audience which was no longer satisfied with the echoing of bourgeois sentiments. It is now apparent that the princely benefactors who stimulated poets to the production of exalted verse were indirectly responsible for refinement of texts in secular music. Since the chief composers of *frottole* were court musicians by profession, their masters and mistresses readily imposed upon them the shifting dictates of literary fashion. Most credit for the change in musical taste is due to the Marchioness of Mantua, Isabella d'Este, and to the talented men of letters both in and out of her immediate circle whose verses she chose to be sung. Their contributions can only be evaluated, however, when compared with the prevalent standards of proletarian rhymes. As far as possible, therefore, the musical texts of all noteworthy poets, both those who specialized in pseudo-plebian verse and those Petrarchans who aspired to a nobler form of art, will be identified here.

---

[19] *Fioretti di frottole* ... *Lib. II* (Napoli), f. LXX, reprinted in part by Charles Van den Borren, in Lavignac's *Encyclopédie* ... II[5] (Paris: Delagrave, 1930), 3049, in full by Gotti in his *Vita di Michelangelo Buonarotti* (Firenze: 1876), II, 99 ff. For an illuminating discussion of the transition, see G. Cesari, "Le origini del madrigale musicale cinquecentesco," *Rivista Musicale Italiana,* XIX, 1, 2 (1912), 1–34, 380–428.

[20] *Madrigali de diversi musici libro primo de la serena.* The alto part-book only of this, an earlier edition of Vogel, 1533[1], in Seville, Biblioteca Colombina. See Jeppesen, "Die neuentdeckten Bücher der Lauden des Ottaviano dei Petrucci," *Zeitschrift f. Musikwissenschaft,* XII, 2 (Nov., 1929), 77.

II. ISABELLA D'ESTE AND MUSICAL POETRY; THE BARZELLETTE OF DEL CARRETTO AND GAMBARA

ONE OF THE shining lights of the Renaissance, Isabella d'Este—of whom Ariosto wrote, *Quella d'opere illustri e di be' studi amica, ... liberale e magnanima Isabella*[1]—was a patroness of literature, the pictorial arts, and music. An intimate of most Italian poets whose productivity falls within the span of years allotted to the *frottola,* she corresponded with them all, especially with those who were members of her immediate circle, requesting their newly composed verses so regularly that her insistence amounted almost to an obsession. Part of this correspondence is directly related to musical composition, and will be analyzed in conjunction with the contributions of individual poets.

It was Isabella's habit to require of her musicians fitting accompaniments to the newly acquired rhymes, with resulting benefit to the literature of secular song. Since two of the foremost composers of *frottole,* Marchetto Cara[2] and Bartolomeo Tromboncino,[3] were in her service, the court at Mantua has been considered the chief fount of this music. The works of both singers reflect the literary tastes of their mistress; hence they form a primary source for our study of changing quality in musical texts.

Isabella was herself a talented performer on the clavichord and the lute, which she had been taught to play by the eminent lutenist, Angelo Testagrossa. Frequent references to the beauty of her voice (see p. 28) bear witness to the pedagogical skill of her vocal instructor, the Flemish composer Johannes Martini.[4] So great was her love of music that she ordered a design of clefs, time signatures, and repeat marks sculptured into the wall of her room, and even had the emblems embroidered on one of her gala dresses.[5]

Since Isabella was possessed of so much musical talent, it seems very natural that poetry and music were inseparably linked in her mind. Lyrical verses were

---

[1] *Orlando Furioso,* XIII, 59.

[2] Cara was a favorite of the Mantuan court as early as 1495, remaining there in the capacity of singer and composer and obtaining local citizenship in 1525. Isabella granted him many favors, including country estates and a Mantuan house, and, in 1512, one of her court ladies (named Leali) for a wife. Cara died *ca.* 1527. See A. Bertolotti, *Musici alla corte dei Gonzaga in Mantova del sec. XIV–XVIII* (Milano, 1890), p. 20. Castiglione pays tribute to Cara's musicianship in his *Cortegiano* (*ed. cit.,* p. 50) with these words: "Nor does our friend Marchetto Cara move us less by his singing but with a gentler harmony; because he softens and penetrates our souls by placid means and full of plaintive sweetness, gently stirring them to sweet emotion."

[3] Tromboncino was born in Verona, the son of Bernardino Piffaro, who entered Mantuan service in 1487. Bartolomeo was also in the employ of the Gonzagas by 1495, but in this year he left and followed his father to Venice, being subsequently readmitted to the Mantuan court upon his parent's request. He married a certain Antonia Mantovano, and, finding her unfaithful, in July, 1499, he stabbed both his wife and her paramour to death. In disgrace at court because of this act, he was too competent a composer to remain long out of favor. In 1513 he seems definitely to have left Isabella's service, transferring to the court at Ferrara (Bertolotti, *op. cit.,* p. 12, 20).

[4] A selection of his motets is in *Das Chorwerk,* ed. Fr. Blume, Heft 46 (Wolfenbüttel-Berlin: Kallmeyer, 1937).

[5] A. Luzio and R. Renier, "Coltura e relazioni letterarie d'Isabella d'Este," *Giorn. Stor.,* XXXIII (1899), 51.

thoroughly enjoyable to her only when they were sung to the lute or the clavichord, and bedecked with an accompaniment which could readily be provided by her master frottolists. When she wished to send a gift of newly composed verses to a literary-minded friend, she did so by means of a musical courier. Thus Marco Cara was dispatched to the podestà of Verona, Bernardo Bembo, with instructions to sing the tribute offered, musical verses concerning Venus and Cupid.[6]

Of the poets who specialized in popular, pseudo-plebeian verse, the Marquis Galeotto del Carretto (d. 1531) was perhaps most closely linked to Isabella d'Este and her company of artists. His more ambitious poetry consists largely of sonnets replete with the usual Petrarchisms, but his *barzellette* are spontaneous and original, and because of these qualities were often set to music. Galeotto seems to have made a regular practice of sending his verses to Isabella for her approval, although at first he modestly hesitated to submit rhymes to such a *connoisseuse*.[7] The Marchioness was always delighted with them, however, and regularly gave them to Tromboncino or Cara to be harmonized. One of several proofs of this is the letter sent by Galeotto to Isabella on January 29, 1500, which reads in part: "I have just had a communication from your excellency in which you mention receipt of the *barzellette* I sent you through Pelegrino. This pleases me, especially since you gave them to Tromboncino to be set to music."[8] Another letter, published by Rudolph Schwartz,[9] mentions several of the poet's *barzellette* by name: "Your excellency knows that at the time of my departure from Mantua, you promised to send me some of Tromboncino's songs to my *barzellette*, yet I have never received them. I should like the following songs to the *barzellette: Lassa, o donna, i dolci sguardi; Pace ormai, o miei sospiri; Se gran festa me mostrasti; Donna, sai come tuo sono* [Galeotto to Isabella, January 14, 1497]." It can now be determined that the first *frottola* mentioned in the letter was printed by Petrucci in *Lib. VI*, 33; the second may be identical with *Pace hormai che a discoprire* in *Lib. V*, 16; whereas the third, already identified by Schwartz, is in *Lib. V*, 38, and a number of manuscript sources,[10] from one of which it has been transcribed for inclusion in the Appendix (No. 2) of this monograph.

Some additional musical *barzellette* by Galeotto, possibly those to which he refers in the first letter quoted above, are the following: *Poi che amor con dritta fè*,[11] which was published by Petrucci in *Lib. III*, 2; Tromboncino's set-

[6] See Bembo's letter of September 2, 1502, in V. Cian, "Pietro Bembo e Isabella d'Este Gonzaga," *Giorn. Stor.*, IX (1887), 90.

[7] Rodolfo Renier, "Saggio di rime inedite di Galeotto del Carretto," *Giorn. Stor.*, VI (1885), 238 n.

[8] V. Promis, "Galeotto del Carretto ed alcune sue lettere," *Curiosità e ricerche di storia subalpina*, III (1876), 47–48.

[9] "Die Frottole im 15. Jahrhundert," *Viertelj. f. Musikw.*, II (1886), 450.

[10] Milano, Bibl. Trivulziana, MS 55, no. 45 (see Jeppesen, "Ueber einige unbekannte Frottolenhandschriften," *Acta Mus.*, XI, 91), and Firenze, R. Ist. Mus., MS B 2441, fol. 25' (see "Catalogo delle opere musicali ... esistenti ... nelle biblioteche e negli archivi pubblici e privati d'Italia, Città di Firenze: Bibl. della R. Conserv. di Musica," *Bollettino dell'Associazione dei Musicologi Italiani*, Ser. IV, Vol. 1, Puntata XVIII (Parma, 1929), pp. 248–249. The text published by G. Manacorda, "Galeotto del Carretto," p. 125.

[11] Text in A. G. Spinelli, "Galeotto del Carretto, poesie inedite," *Atti e Memorie della Società Stor. Savonese*, I (1888), 471.

ting of *Son disposto in tutto hormai*,[12] deemed worthy of inclusion in Antico's *Canzoni nove*, no. 15; and the well-known *Chi ben ama, tardi oblia*, the music of which is retained for us in manuscript only.[13]

In a Venetian manuscript may be found the musical embellishment to a Del Carrettian poem in a more elegant pattern, the *canzone* beginning:

> *Da poi longe fatiche et longi affanni,*
> *Da poi longo mio amor, alma mia dea,*
> *In qualche loco almen pur mi credea*
> *Potervi in parte dir delli miei danni;*
> *Se non che morte coi suoi duri inganni,*
> *Nemica espressa di ciascun mio bene,*
> *Fuora di tanta spene,*
> *Contra ragion m'ha tolto et misso a tale*
> *Che spesso quella chiamo per men male.*[14]

Veronica Gambara (1485–1550) was one of the first ladies of the Italian Renaissance, a poetess whose mature compositions were formally exquisite, although lacking in warmth and genuineness of feeling. During her youth she also contributed to the literature of the *frottola* with the *barzelletta* beginning:

> *(H)or passata è la speranza,*
> *Che mi tenni un tempo ardendo;*
> *Men mi duol, poichè io comprendo*
> *Nulla cosa aver costanza.*
> *(H)or passata è la speranza.*[15]

This was printed by Petrucci in his *Lib. V*, 7, when Veronica was only twenty, or some time before her marriage. The years with her beloved husband, Gilberto, were blissfully happy ones, but her romance ended cruelly with his death in 1518. Just as Petrarca had obtained in his unrequited love for Laura a poetical theme which was to remain valid for all his life, so did Veronica dedicate her talent to a glorification of her passion for her husband, drawing again and again upon the circumstances of her marital life and its tragic conclusion for the subject matter of her poetry. Knowledge of these facts, but not of Petrucci's volume (1505), prompts Luigi Tonelli[16] to quote in a recent book the *barzelletta* given above, with an accompanying, rhapsodic statement that it admirably illustrates Veronica's constancy of mood after Gilberto's death, a mood of resigned sorrow. Even as a girl Veronica had been on friendly terms with the family d'Este, and particularly with Isabella, with whom she had corresponded as early as 1503.[17] It is therefore entirely possible that one of the Mantuan composers, Tromboncino or Cara, set the *barzelletta* to music, since it was melancholically amorous in the approved, popular manner, and would surely have pleased the Marchioness had it been submitted to her.

[12] Text in G. Manacorda, *op. cit.*, p. 124.

[13] Milano, Bibl. Trivulz., MS 55, no. 66. Text in R. Renier, *Giorn. Stor.*, VI, 251, and in L. Tonelli, *L'amore nella poesia e nel pensiero del Rinascimento* (Firenze: Sansoni, 1933), p. 27.

[14] G. Manacorda, *op. cit.*, pp. 123–124. Music in the Bibl. Marciana, MSS Italiani Cl. IV, No. 1795–1798, no. 11.

[15] Veronica Gambara, *Rime e lettere*, ed. P. M. Chiappetti (Firenze, 1879), pp. 58–60.

[16] *Op. cit.*, p. 90.

[17] R. Renier, in the Rassegna Bibliografica, *Giorn. Stor.*, XIV (1889), 442.

III. SERAFINO, PRINCE OF STRAMBOTTISTS, AND HIS SCHOOL

A CELEBRATED IMPROVISATOR of popular verse, whose works are represented in the earlier prints and manuscripts of *frottole* much more often than those of any identifiable contemporary, was Serafino de' Ciminelli dall'Aquila (Aquilano), who lived from 1466 to 1500. His biography was written shortly after his death by a friend, Vincenzo Collo, called *Il Calmeta*, himself a well-known rhymster whose *strambotto, La faza obscura e gli occhi humidi e bassi* may be found harmonized in a Milanese manuscript.[1] Calmeta (d. 1508), secretary to Beatrice, Duchess of Milan, remained in close relationship with the literary circles at Mantua and Urbino, where he was held in such esteem that Castiglione included him as an interlocutor in the *Cortegiano*.

According to the biography,[2] Serafino learned the rudiments of musical composition from a certain Guillaume the Fleming (Guillaume Garnier) at Naples, and profited so much from the latter's erudition that he soon had no Italian peer in the improvisation of songs. Returning to Aquila about 1480, he applied himself for three years to the memorizing of Petrarca's sonnets, *canzoni*, and *trionfi*, singing them beautifully to his own accompaniment on the lute. In doing this he was preparing himself for a lucrative profession, since those who could boast both musical and poetical talents were assured of court positions as entertaining improvisators. To mention only two of the many virtuosi who were thus employed at the close of the *quattrocento*, the blind poets Giovanni Cieco di Parma and Francesco Cieco di Ferrara—he who wrote the famous epic poem *Il Mambriano*, which served as a model for Ariosto's *Orlando Furioso*,—both sang and accompanied their own verses for the delectation of the court at Ferrara.[3]

Transferring to Rome, Serafino was now admitted into the service of Cardinal Ascanio Sforza, the same Ascanio who employed Josquin des Prés and the painter Pinturicchio. From some of the poet's verses written during the following years, we learn that the Cardinal was an unpleasant and hated master. For this reason, the famous anecdote concerning the origin of Josquin's mass *La, sol, fa, re, mi*, which has been prefaced to the authoritative edition of the composition,[4] probably refers also to Ascanio. The tale goes as follows: Josquin, seeking a favor, had been promised it over and over again by his

---

[1] Bibl. Trivulz., MS 55, fol. 20'–21. The text is ascribed to Vincentii in Cod. Vat. Urb. 729, see G. Zannoni, "Strambotti inedite del sec. XV," *Rendiconti dell'Accademia dei Lincei*, Ser. V, I (1892), 384; and in Firenze, Bibl. Naz., MS Magl. II.X.54, see G. Mazzatinti, *Inventarii dei MSS delle biblioteche d'Italia*, XII (Forli: 1902–1903), 44. Dr. Einstein informs me that the text to Tromboncino's *Naque al mondo per amare* (*Lib. III*, 6) may be found in the *Compendio de cose nove, de V. Calmeta et altri auctori ...* (Venetia: Manfredo de Monteferrato, 1508).

[2] *Vita del facondo poeta vulgare Seraphino Aquilano*, in *Collettanee grece, latine e vulgari ...* (Bologna, 1504); modern reprint in M. Menghini, *Le rime di Serafino de' Ciminelli dall'Aquila* (Bologna, 1894), pp. 1–15.

[3] G. Bertoni, "Il Cieco di Ferrara e altri improvvisatori alla corte d'Este," *Giorn. Stor.*, XCIV (1929), 271 ff.

[4] *Werken van Josquin des Prés*, uitg. A. Smijers; Vereeniging voor Nederlandsche Muziekgeschiedenis, XI. Aflevering (Amsterdam: Alsbach, 1926).

patron, who said *"Lascia fare mi"* each time the request was repeated. Finally, tiring of such meaningless assurances, Des Prés composed a mass using as *cantus firmus* the solmization tones *la, sol, fa, re, mi*, derived from the nobleman's rejoinder, and then presented it to the procrastinator. Perhaps the story is true, but there is reason to believe that the theme of Josquin's mass was the result of an inspiration from another source, the popular *barzelletta* beginning:

> *Lassa far a mi, lassa far a mi;*
> *Non ti curare, lassa far a mi. ...*

and ending:

> *Di dir: lassa far a mi*
> *Son le note di cantori,*
> *Dicon la, re, fa, sol, mi.*[5]

The discovery by Knud Jeppesen[6] of a *quodlibet* in which the song *Lassa fare a mi* is quoted may be taken as further evidence that these verses in musical setting were widely disseminated. To speculate further and thus link both hypotheses, it is entirely possible that Serafino himself became aware of his friend Josquin's plight and wrote the *barzelletta* as a literary barb aimed at Ascanio. Seen in this light, other phrases of the poem become particularly pertinent, to wit:

> "Your saying of: 'Leave it to me'
> Allows your tongue to lie; ...
> One no longer puts any faith
> In your: 'Leave it to me.' "

One need but recall another poem by Serafino, the often-printed sonnet *Ad Jusquino, suo compagno musico d'Ascanio,*[7] in which he also sympathizes with the composer and makes pointed remarks about the Cardinal and his kind. Here he advises Josquin to cease envying the nobles with their fine clothes, and compares them with wood, which of necessity needs decoration, but Des Prés with fine silver and gold. Also, he warns that the moods of the elite are capricious, and their favor most transitory.

In 1490 Serafino accompanied the Cardinal on a visit to Lodovico Sforza's court in Milan, where he heard a Neapolitan singer, Andrea Coscia by name, perform the exquisite *strambotti* of a celebrated Spanish virtuoso, Benedetto Gareth (*Il Chariteo*). Gareth, who had spent most of his life in the service of the Spanish princes at Naples, was not only a secretary of state and the intimate friend of Ferdinand of Aragon, but a genial writer of amorous and political poetry as well. Possessed of a fine voice, Chariteo also improvised the musical accompaniment to his verses, one of which, the *strambotto* beginning:

> *Amando e desiando, io vivo, e sento*
> *La doglia, che si sente nel morire.*
> *Amor viver mi fa sempre in tormento,*
> *Nè vol ch'io viva, nè mi vol finire,*[8]

was printed by Petrucci with the poet's own harmonization (*Lib. IX,* fol. 56).

---

[5] Menghini, *op. cit.,* pp. 35–38.

[6] "Ueber einige unbekannte Frottolenhandschriften," *Acta Mus.,* XI, 102, n. 17.

[7] See Fétis, *Biographie universelle des musiciens* (2° ed.; Paris, 1875), II, 475; and Menghini, *op. cit.,* p. 112.

[8] E. Percopo, *Le rime del Chariteo* (Napoli, 1892), II, 453.

Serafino was so deeply impressed by the polish and charm of the Spaniard's rhymes that he immediately applied himself to the composition of *strambotti,* which were to bring him great fame. One of these, *Tu dormi, io veghio e vo spargendo i passi* (subsequently set to music by Tromboncino, see p. 18), is a scarcely veiled adaptation of Chariteo's *Tu dormi, e Amor veglia per mio danno,*[9] thus serving as documentary evidence of Aquilano's indebtedness.

Returning to Rome, Serafino's reputation as an improvisator of amorous lyrics increased apace, according to Calmeta, until the time came when all new *strambotti,* even those composed by other authors, were attributed to him. Many of these are retained for us in anonymous tonal settings, a circumstance lending credence to the hypothesis that here in musical notation are Serafino's own extempore performances. Much of the poet's success was due to his manner of delivery, an ardent recitation, according to Calmeta, in which music and poetry were so ideally combined and balanced that the hearts of all his listeners were touched, whether they were learned aristocrats, dilettantes, or of the common herd.

At least three of Aquilano's *strambotti* were included in Petrucci's fourth book (now available in modern transcription) :[10] No. 41, *La nocte aquieta ogni (fiero) animale,*[11] No. 78, *Quando, per darme nel languir conforto,*[12] and No. 47, *Non ti smarir, cor mio, va passo passo.*[13] The last named is unique because of its (for that time) un-Italian texture: one voice, the tenor, illustrates a canonic device characteristic of contemporary northern music—its second section is to be read in retrograde fashion, as an alternate or perhaps a companion to the initium. In view of Serafino's friendship with Josquin, *Non ti smarir* may well have been the fruit of artistic collaboration between the two masters. The use of a so-called "Netherlandish canonic trick" certainly points in that direction.

Still other examples of the poet's *strambotti* are printed in Petrucci's *Lib. IX,* fol. 27: *Gratia, poi che virtù fa l'omo grato,*[14] and in *Lib. XI,* no. 2: *Se un pone un fragil vetro in megio al foco,*[15] the latter composed by Honofrius Patavinus. Of the several so-called literary verse forms employed occasionally by Serafino, none seems to have had the musical significance of the

---

[9] *Ibid.,* II, 445.

[10] Schwartz, *Ottaviano Petrucci, Frottole, Buch I und IV,* Pub. ält. Musik, VIII.

[11] "Fiero" according to MS Panc. 27, fol. 33 (Firenze, Bibl. Naz. Centr.), and to the literary sources. The poem is ascribed to Serafino in Paris, Bibl. Nat., Cod. Ital. 1543, see G. Mazzatinti, *Inventario dei MSS italiani delle biblioteche di Francia* (Roma, 1887), II, 536; and in the Venetian edition of his rhymes (1505).

[12] Serafino, according to the Cod. Ital. 1543, Paris, Bibl. Nat., see Mazzatinti, *Inventario ... Francia,* II, 539; and the edition of his poems by Philippo di Giunta (Firenze, 1516), fol. 141'.

[13] Ascribed to Serafino in Cod. Mazarin 7786, Paris, Bibl. Nat., see Mazzatinti, *Inventario ... Francia,* II, 192. There is an entirely different musical arrangement of the poem in Milano, Bibl. Trivulz., MS 55, fol. 44'–45.

[14] Serafino, according to Cod. Vat. 5170, no. 209, see Menghini, "Poesie inedite del sec. XV," *Rassegna Bibliografica della Letteratura Italiana,* III (1895), 25; and Giunta's edition (1516), no. 433.

[15] In Joh. Besicken's second ed. of Serafino's rhymes (Roma, 1503), see Menghini, *Le rime di Serafino ...* (Bologna, 1894), I, xi. The second volume of Menghini's publication, which was to have contained the *strambotti* and other popular verse forms, has not as yet been printed.

strambotto. To my knowledge, only one specimen of his more cultivated poetry was set to music by the frottolists, the *capitolo, Ben ti puoi lucidar, candida aurora.*[16] This was harmonized by E. Romanus and printed in a somewhat later collection, Antico's *Frottole libro quarto,* Venice, 1520.

A goodly number of *strambotti* which were current throughout Italy under Serafino's name may be discovered in musical manuscripts compiled about 1500. The contents of one such collection (now in the British Museum) have been listed in detail by Jeppesen. An examination of this register of *capoversi,* made more usable through supplementary texts obligingly furnished by Dr. Alfred Einstein, shows that an entire section of the manuscript is devoted to Aquilano's *strambotti,*[17] from No. 7, *Tu dormi, io veghio* (see pp. 14 and 18), to No. 18, *Voi che passate qui* (see p. 22, n. 15, where ascriptions to both Pulci and Serafino are cited). With the possible exception of No. 10, *Lo infermo alhor,* the authorship of which could not readily be determined, these were all laid to Serafino's door by enthusiastic admirers, whether he actually penned them or not.

A codex in the Trivulziana, Milan (MS 55), contains several additional *strambotti* by Aquilano, to wit: the initial component, *Gridan vostri occhi al cor mio: fora, fora,*[18] as well as (No. 18) *Non te stimar se a te ciascun s'ar rende,*[19] (No. 43) *Non te smarir, cor mio, va passo passo* in a musical arrangement distinct from that published by Petrucci (see p. 14), (No. 51) *Del mio amar grande et del tuo amor pocho,*[20] and (No. 64) *Ahy lasso, a quante fiere*

[16] The seventh *capitolo* in Giunta's edition of Serafino's rhymes (1516), fol. 81'.

[17] See Jeppesen, "Ueber einige unbekannte Frottolenhandschriften," *Acta Mus.,* XI, 81 ff. (No. 8), *Non ti smarir, cor mio* (see p. 14 above); (No. 9) *Peregrinando vo per mio destino:* Serafino according to Cod. Vat. 5170, no. 95, see Menghini, "Poesie inedite ... ," *Rass. Bibl. d. Lett. Ital.* III, 22; also Besicken's first ed. of the poet's rhymes (Roma: 1502), no. 35; and Cod. Vat. Urb. 729, no. 236, see G. Zannoni, *op. cit.,* p. 385; (No. 11) *Quanto la fiama è più forte renchiusa:* Serafino in Bazaleri's ed. of his poems (Bologna, 1504), no. 224, but ascribed to Vincentii in Cod. Vat. 5170, see Menghini, "Poesie inedite ... ," p. 23; (No. 12) *Se'l pastor con affanno:* Serafino in Giunta's ed. (1516), fol. 159', but G. Zocholi in Cod. Vat. Urb. 729, no. 125, see Zannoni, *op. cit.,* p. 382; (No. 13) *Rendi quella alma, insidiosa morte:* Serafino in Giunta's ed., fol. 160, but Marco Lauredani in Cod. Vat. Urb. 729, no. 210, see Zannoni, *op. cit.,* p. 384; (No. 14) *Vivo sol di mirarti, o dura impresa:* Serafino in Cod. Magl. II.X.54, Firenze, Bibl. Naz., see Mazzatinti, *Inventarii ... d'Italia,* XII (Forli, 1902–1903), 46; (No. 15) *Spesso nascosti stan tra vaghi fiori:* Serafino in Besicken's ed. (1502), no. 40, and in Cod. Magl. II.X.54, see Mazzatinti, *Inventarii ... d'Italia,* XII, 44; (No. 16) *Spesso nel mezo d'un bel fabricare:* Serafino in Besicken's ed. (1502), no. 22, in Giunta's ed. (1516), fol. 119', in Cod. Ital. 1543, Paris, Bibl. Nat., see Mazzatinti, *Inventario ... Francia* (Roma, 1887), II, 537, and in Cod. Vat. Urb. 729, no. 254, see Zannoni, *op. cit.,* p. 386; (No. 17) *Guardando alli ochi toi, mancar mi sento:* Serafino in Besicken's ed. (1502), no. 33, and in Cod. Magl. II.X.54, see Mazzatinti, *Inventarii ... d'Italia,* XII, 44.

[18] See Jeppesen, "Ueber einige unbekannte Frottolenhandschriften," *Acta Mus.,* XI, 88 ff. Also in Modena, Bibl. Estense, MS a.F.9.9, fol. 31, see "Catálogo ... Città di Modena," *Bollettino dell'Assoc. dei Musicologi Italiani,* Ser. VIII (Parma, 1916–1924), pp. 533–534. The poem ascribed to Serafino in Besicken's ed. (1502), no. 41; in Giunta's ed. (1516), fol. 119'; in Cod. Vat. 5170, no. 208, see Menghini, "Poesie inedite ... ," p. 25; and in Cod. Vat. Urb. 729, no. 43, see Zannoni, *op. cit.,* p. 379. The aforementioned Modenese MS also contains the musical version of *Se'l zappator el giorno s'affatica,* a *strambotto* attributed to Serafino in Giunta's ed., fol. 126', also in Cod. Vat. Urb. 729, no. 144, see Zannoni, *op. cit.,* p. 382.

[19] In Giunta's ed. of Serafino's verses (1516), fol. 146.

[20] Serafino in Cod. Vat. Urb. 729, no. 6, see Zannoni, *op. cit.,* p. 377; also in MS Magl. II.X.54, see Mazzatinti, *Inventarii ... d'Italia,* XII, 46; and in Cod. Ital. 1543, Paris, Bibl. Nat., see Mazzatinti, *Inventario ... Francia,* II, 539.

la sete toglio.[21] The second of these is No. 3 in the musical Appendix to this monograph, and the last three appear in facsimile on the frontispiece. Of the several other sources, mention of two Florentine manuscripts must temporarily suffice. The *strambotti, Disperso per lo mundo pelegrino* and *Soffrire son disposto ogni tormento,*[22] are contained in the MS Panc. 27, Bibl. Naz., fol. 1 and 13′ respectively, while another, reminiscent of Chariteo, is entitled *Ecco la nocte, e'l sol soi raggi absconde*[23] and may be found set to music by Bartholomeus the Florentine organist, in MS B 2440, R. Istituto Musicale.

Having acquired an enviable reputation in Rome, Serafino proceeded to Naples, where he established himself at Ferdinand's court and remained for three years. Naples was a focal point for many artists, both Italian and Spanish, including Aquilano's erstwhile model Chariteo and the eminent humanist Jacopo Sannazzaro, and as such was perhaps the chief clearing house for the literature and music of both Mediterranean countries. Prima facie evidence of an interrelationship between the *frottola* and Spanish secular vocal music is afforded by the unmistakable traces of mutual infiltration between the chief collections of both, Petrucci's publications on the one hand and the *Cancionero musical*[24] on the other.

In the Iberian collection there are no less than eight specimens of *frottole,*[25] all but one of which appeared simultaneously in Petrucci's volumes. Most significant of these is No. 80, Tromboncino's setting of Serafino's *barzelletta, Vox clamantis in deserto,*[26] printed by Petrucci in *Lib. III,* 58. That the scribe of the Spanish codex did not copy directly from Petrucci is evident from the textual and musical differences between the two sources. Perhaps certain Spanish visitors who on occasion were allowed to enjoy and admire Serafino's virtuosity, or who were cognizant of his renown even after his stay at Naples had ended, carried the *Vox clamantis* and other amorous verses back home with them.

Tromboncino, the most versatile and progressive of the frottolists, was obviously subjected to reciprocal influences when he set this *barzelletta.*

---

[21] Ascribed to Serafino in Besicken's ed. (1502), no. 166, and in MS Magl. II.X.54, see Mazzatinti, *Inventarii ... d'Italia,* XII, 44.

[22] Serafino in Cod. Vat. 5170, nos. 194 and 174 respectively, see Menghini, "Poesie inedite ...," p. 24.

[23] Attributed to Serafino in Cod. Oliveriano 54, see A. Saviotti, "Rime inedite del sec. XV," *Propugnatore,* n.s., V (1892), 322; and in Cod. Magl. II.X.54, see Mazzatinti, *Inventarii ... d'Italia,* XII, 44.

[24] Francisco Barbieri, ed., *Cancionero musical de los siglos XV y XVI* (Madrid, 1890).

[25] (No. 63) *Dolce, amoroso focho* (Petrucci, *Lib. V,* fol. 32′–33; also London, Brit. Mus., MS Egerton 3051, no. 45, etc., see Jeppesen, "Ueber einige unbekannte Frottolenhandschriften," *Acta Mus.,* XI, 84); (No. 68) Josquin's *In te, domine, speravi* (*Lib. I,* no. 56, see Schwartz, *Ottaviano Petrucci ...,* Pub. ält. Mus., VIII, 37); (No. 73) *L'amor, donna, ch'io te porto* (*Lib. VII,* fol. 18′); (No. 78) *De, fosse la qui mecho* (*Lib. VI,* fol. 49; printed by Barbieri, *op. cit.,* p. 606, to illustrate numerous variants); (No. 124) *Guarda, donna, el mio tormento* (*Lib. II,* fol. 39′–40; also MS Egerton 3051, no. 1, etc., see Jeppesen, "Ueber einige unbekannte Frottolenhandschriften," *Acta Mus.,* XI, 82); (No. 261) Jo. Brocchus' *Io mi voglio lamentare* (*Lib. III,* fol. 28, and Firenze, Bibl. Naz., MS Panc. 27, fol. 42); (No. 266) *Perchè me fuge, amore.*

[26] Giunta's ed. of Serafino's rhymes (1516), no. 15.

Nunqua fu pena magiore,
Ne tormento tanto strano,
Che vederse in desfavore,
E haver speso el tempo invano,[27]

for in it he utilized as point of departure the first two lines of Don García
Álvarez de Toledo, the Duke de Alba's Spanish poem, beginning:

Nunca fué pena mayor,
Nin tormento tan extraño,
Que iguale con el dolor
Que rescibo del engaño.

These verses were in everyone's mouth, not only on the Spanish peninsula,
where the Portuguese dramatist Gil Vicente quoted them in his plays (by
Venus in *Las cortes de Jupiter,* and by Peregrino in *Fragoa d'Amor*), but
throughout the rest of Europe in a musical setting by Juan Urrede (Wrede)
which, significantly enough, was included in the *Cancionero musical* as its
initial component, and was printed by Petrucci (with the addition of a fourth
voice-part) in the *Odhecaton,*[28] fol. 6'–7. Thus one may note another instance
of partial correspondence between the Spanish collection and Petrucci's
editions. Wrede's composition served also as the model for masses by Pierre
de la Rue, composed during a trip to Spain (1501–1503) in the suite of Philip
the Fair, and by **Franc. Penalosa,** chapel singer of Ferdinand and Isabella.

Many of the circumstances relating to contemporary musical interchange
between Spain and Italy remain to be determined, but it can no longer be
disputed that a deep-seated relationship existed between the tonal arts of both
lands. The technique evident in most of the music of the *Cancionero,* that
composed before the influence of Netherlandish polyphony made itself felt,
is similar to that used in the Italian *frottola,* laud, and carnival chant (elements of which were analyzed on pp. 3–4). The corresponding Spanish characteristics may be summarized as follows: (*a*) Most songs are homophonic
and isometric in texture, that is, similar to the conductus or simple hymn.
The several voices are conceived as a rhythmic unit, proceed from measure
to measure in approximately parallel fashion, with essentially similar note
values, and usually begin simultaneously after a pause. Polyphonic imitation
is rare, and incidental when it does occur. (*b*) The length of a musical phrase
is entirely dependent upon the text, that is, all voices generally come to a
momentary halt at the end of each line of poetry. (*c*) The chief melody is in
the upper voice, which in its preference for diatonic steps or repetitions of the
same tone seems always to have been written in compliance with demands
for the utmost in clarity of enunciation and comprehensibility. A further

[27] Petrucci, *Lib. III,* fol. 55; Firenze, R. Ist. Mus., MS B 2440, no. 25; see "Catalogo ...
Città di Firenze," *Boll. dell'Assoc. dei Musicologi Italiani,* Ser. IV, I (Parma, 1929),
243–244.

[28] (Venice, 1501); facsimile edition by the *Bollettino Bibliografico Musicale* (Milano,
1932). Modern reprints of the three-voice version in E. van der Straeten, *La Musique aux
Pays-Bas ...* (Bruxelles, 1867–1888), VIII, 454; and in Barbieri, *op. cit.,* p. 233.

point of similarity in musical usage is the insertion of *villancicos* or *frottole* into the dramatic representations of each country.[29]

To return to Serafino, the wandering minstrel left Naples and visited Mantua for the first time in December, 1494,[30] finding in Isabella a patroness who rewarded virtuosi munificently. During subsequent years, he spent much time at the Mantuan court, delighting the Marchioness with his improvisations. Whenever he was required to be absent, he continued to send his verses to her by courier,[31] whereupon Tromboncino or Cara were asked to provide the musical settings. The former must have harmonized many of Serafino's poems, but of these only two could be accurately identified, the *strambotto, Tu dormi, io veghio e vo spargendo i passi*,[32] and the *barzelletta, Vox clamantis in deserto* (see above, p. 16).

As might be expected, Serafino's style was imitated by a host of minor poets, several of whom contributed light and agreeable verses to the literature of secular vocal music. Mention has already been made of one such disciple, Calmeta (see p. 12). Another was Bartolomeo Cavassico (1480–1555), a rhymester whose verses were a judicious combination of plebeian sentiments and the inevitable Petrarchisms. One of his lyrics, classified by Petrucci as an ode, may be found in the latter's *Lib. II*, fol. 27′, set by P. Cesena of Verona. Its first strophe is an admirable illustration of the short, rollicking lines so dear to a simple audience:

> *O dolce diva mia,*
> *Unica mia signora,*
> *Resta, chè gionto è l'hora*
> *Del partire.*[33]

A well-known poet and improvisator, with a remarkable memory for the recitation of verses, was Panfilo Sassi (Sasso de' Sassi, *ca.* 1455–1527). In seclusion near Verona for most of his creative life, he nevertheless expressed in his *strambotti* that artificiality of sentiment and forced gentility peculiar to the poets who frequented the courts of central and northern Italy. Two of Panfilo's *strambotti* may be found set to music anonymously in a Modenese MS: *Gridati, tutti amanti: al fuocho, al fuocho*[34] and *La vecchiarella peregrina*

---

[29] See sec. vi; also Gilbert Chase, "Origins of the Lyric Theatre in Spain," *Musical Quarterly*, XXV, 3 (July, 1939), 292–305; and Adolfo Salazar, *Music in the Primitive Spanish Theatre before Lope de Vega*, Papers ... of the American Musicological Society at the Annual Meeting, Washington, D. C. ... 1938 (printed by the Society, 1940), pp. 94–108.

[30] A. Luzio and R. Renier, "Coltura e relazioni letterarie d'Isabella d'Este," *Giorn. Stor.*, XL (1902), 330, n. 5.

[31] Luzio and Renier, *Mantova e Urbino: Isabella d'Este ed Elisabetta Gonzaga nelle relazioni famigliari e nelle vicende politiche* (Torino, 1893), pp. 90–91.

[32] Serafino according to the Cod. Vat. 5170, no. 205, see Menghini, "Poesie inedite ... ," p. 25; and Besicken's first ed. (1502), no. 118. The music in Petrucci's *Lib. VI*, 9; Brit. Mus., MS Egerton 3051, no. 7; Vogel, 1509¹, 22 (B.T.).

[33] V. Cian, *Le rime di Bartolomeo Cavassico*, Scelta di curiosità letterarie, vv. 246, 247 (Bologna, 1893–1894), II, 306.

[34] Bibl. Est., MS a.F.9.9, fol. 11′–12; also in Milano, Bibl. Trivulz., MS 55, no. 30, with but an incomplete version of the text. The poem published by Sev. Ferrari, *Biblioteca di letteratura popolare italiana* (Firenze, 1882), I, 284.

e stanca.[35] Perhaps one may again assume that these are Sassi's own extemporary harmonizations.

Still another rhymester who paid court to Serafino, Cinthio d'Ancona by name, was renowned during a few decades of the period under discussion, as may be seen from contemporary verses which list him in the same category with poets of recognized genius:

> *Sannazzar, Caracciolo e Cariteo,*
> *Laur de' Medici e il Politiano,*
> *Cinthio d'Ancona e il chiaro Tebaldeo ...*
> *Di laur coronati eccelsi e degni.*[36]

Cinthio's *strambotto* beginning *Vedo sdegnato amor, crudel e fero,* in a setting by the Venetian organist Fr. Ana, is printed in Petrucci's *Lib. IV,* no. 18.[37]

These virtuosi, and numerous others who have remained in total obscurity, were in attendance upon the recognized leader among improvisators, Serafino, he who so completely established the prevailing taste in popular verse that the final years of his life have appropriately been called "the age of Serafino" in Italian literature. We have seen, however, that the effectiveness of his verses depended to a great extent upon their musical accompaniment, which was not merely an embellishment, but an essential part of the poet's original conception. In tracing the historical development of Italian music, one must therefore reserve for Aquilano a place of honor equal in importance to the one he holds in poetry. Even if he and his followers did not themselves always compose both *"cantus et verba"* to the *frottola,* Serafino's importance as a chief arbiter of musical fashion must still be recognized. The independent harmonizations by professional composers have monopolized the attention of musicologists, who fail to realize that the *frottola* loses its identity when considered solely as music. In essence the form was a synthesis of both arts, unintelligible when divorced from its text, the tone and quality of which had been derived in great measure from Serafino's model verses.

---

[35] Bibl. Est., MS a.F.9.9, fol. 56'–57. Text in A. Cappelli, *Poesie musicali dei secoli XIV, XV e XVI* (Bologna, 1868), p. 59; in Ferrari, *op. cit.,* I, 278; and in Tonelli, *L'Amore nella poesia ...* , p. 18.

[36] From a poem called *Amazonida* by Andrea Stagio d'Ancona, printed at Venice in 1503. See G. Rossi, "Il Codice Estense X.*.34," *Giorn. Stor.,* XXX (1897), 13.

[37] Schwartz, *Ottaviano Petrucci ...* , Pub. ält. Mus., VIII, 57. Also in a number of musical MSS, see Jeppesen, "Ueber einige unbekannte Frottolenhandschriften," *Acta Mus.,* XI, 82, 87, where the variants are listed. The poem is attributed to D'Ancona in the Cod Vat. Urb. 729, no. 63, see Zannoni, *op. cit.,* p. 380.

IV. POPULAR MUSICAL VERSE OF MILANESE
AND FLORENTINE ORIGIN

A NOTED PATRON both of the pictorial arts and of music, Lodovico il Moro, Duke of Milan (1452–1508), called to his court the finest Flemish and Italian singers and instrumentalists. Some were summoned for service in the cathedral choir, and others to provide secular entertainment; among the former was the composer Gaspar Werbecke, whose masses were published by Petrucci in 1506 and whose fame rivaled that of the chief musical authority at Milan, the learned theorist Franchino Gaffurio. The court's insatiable appetite for light music was gratified by the singing of French *chansons*, Spanish *villancicos*, and of course the *barzellette* of native poets, most prominent of whom was the cavalier Gaspare Visconti (1461–1499). A personal friend of Il Moro, Gaspare regaled his intimates with rhymes of love and love's sorrows, all in the favorite pseudo-plebeian style. Although many of his *barzellette* were harmonized by the frottolists, only one can now be identified, *Non mi doglio già d'amore*, printed by Petrucci in a setting by Micha.[1]

The most artistic of poetical efforts in the popular vein were doubtless those of Lorenzo de' Medici (1449–1492) and his circle. It is entirely fitting that the Magnificent One, who participated so fully in the amusements of the Florentine populace, should have written a number of dance songs, *canzoni a ballo*, whose form was usually that of the *barzelletta*. These were intended especially for the crowds who caroused in the streets during the carnival season (between the first of May and St. John's Day, June 24). Plebeian sentiments are expressed by Lorenzo with a delicacy and also a touch of melancholy entirely different from the artificial sorrow of most contemporary literary dilettantes.

The Florentine court was not lacking in musicians who could harmonize these festive *canzoni* in the simple, homophonic style of the *frottola*. The Fleming Heinrich Isaac (Arrigo Tedesco), who came to Florence shortly after the death of the organist Antonio Squarcialupi (1475) and remained there even after Lorenzo's death, regularly wrote the music to his patron's carnival poetry. Many of the *canzoni a ballo* which originated in the Medicean court have been retained for posterity in a Florentine manuscript,[2] the verses having been harmonized by a pleiad of musicians in the patronage of Lorenzo, including the organists Bartholomaeus, Johannes, and Alexander, as well as Bernardo Pisano, Alex. Coppinus, Alex. Agricola, and Pintellus. In one *canzone* beginning:

> *Un dì lieto giamai*
> *Non ebbi, Amor, da poi*
> *Che dalli lacci tuoi mi dislegai*[3]

Lorenzo lightly but melancholically repents having broken with his beloved, since his cup of sorrow is now much fuller than before. This seems to have been

---

[1] Don Michele Pesenti of Verona, *Lib. I*, no. 45; Schwartz, *Ottaviano Petrucci ... *, Pub. ält. Mus., VIII, 33. The text in R. Renier, "Gaspare Visconti," *Archivio Storico Lombardo*, XIII (1886), 538–539; also Tonelli, *L'amore nella poesia ... *, p. 26.

[2] Bibl. Naz., Cod. Magl. XIX, 141. See Federico Ghisi, *I canti carnascialeschi nelle fonti musicali del XV e XVI secolo* (Firenze-Roma: Olschki, 1937), pp. 185–186.

[3] Lorenzo de' Medici, *Opere*, a cura di A. Simioni (Bari, 1914), II, 294.

an especial favorite of the populace, to judge from musical settings by Pisano and by Isaac; both these settings are available in modern print.[4]

Closely related both formally and functionally to the *canzone a ballo* was the Medicean *canto carnascialesco,* or carnival chant, the musical style of which was the same as that of the *frottola*. In a recent book which must of necessity be mentioned here only incidentally, Federico Ghisi treats all aspects of the form in admirable fashion.[5] According to Ghisi's sources, carnival chants were sung by masked groups on floats, who represented various professions and trades. The poetry expressly dedicated to these revelers seems to have first come into prominence during the time of Lorenzo, through whose initiative it grew so much in importance that it has since become an accepted category of verse. Lorenzo's famous *canto dei bericuocolai* (song by the sellers of gingerbread and spicecakes), in a musical setting by Isaac, is said to have been the first of the new genre to be sung at a carnival (*ca.* 1480).[6]

Lorenzo the Magnificent's humorous poem in the simple dialect of the Tuscan countryside (*lingua contadinesca*), entitled *La Nencia da Barberino*,[7] contains a stanza (no. 17) beginning *Nenciozza mia, i' vo' sabato andare sin a Firenze* ... , the initium of which was set to music by Jean Japart and printed by Petrucci in the *Odhecaton*. The mature poet here recaptured the tone and atmosphere of the rustic verses he had heard peasants sing in the Tuscan hills. Written in the popular *ottava rima,* a verse scheme similar to that of the *strambotto,* the lyric is a hymn in praise of a beautiful shepherdess, Nencia. Arnold Schering, apparently unaware of the textual source, assumes that Japart's composition is an instrumental *canzone* and includes it as such in his famous collection of *Beispielen*.[8] The text may be fitted to the uppermost voice, however, leaving, as a probable solution, a composition for solo voice with instrumental accompaniment, in the usual manner of the *frottola*.[9]

Thoroughly devoted to Lorenzo was the genial poet Angiolo Poliziano, he who more than any other established the reputation of the Florentine humanists. Much of his verse in the vulgar tongue represents an attempt at imitation of the popular muse even more studied than were the *canzoni a ballo* of Lorenzo. Poliziano's *rispetti,* or amorous compliments, are as sentimental and unsophisticated as the *strambotti* of the streets, to which they correspond in form. One of these, beginning *Contento in focho (sto) como la fenice,* appears set to music in two of the more important *frottola* manuscripts.[10]

[4] The former in R. Gandolfi, "Intorno al cod. membr. del R. Istituto Musicale di Firenze No. 2440," *Rivista Musicale Italiana,* XVIII (1911), 537 ff., appendix p. 5. Isaac's setting in the authoritative edition of his secular works, *Denkmäler der Tonkunst in Österreich,* XIV, 1 (1907), 44.

[5] *Op. cit.* See also Ghisi, "Carnival Songs and the Origins of the Intermezzo Giocoso," *Musical Quarterly,* XXV, 3 (July, 1939), 325–333, and *Feste musicali della Firenze Medicea (1480–1589), a cura di F. Ghisi* (Firenze: Vallecchi, 1939).

[6] Ghisi, *I canti carnascialeschi* ... , pp. 2, 47.

[7] Lorenzo de' Medici, *op. cit.,* II, 151 ff.

[8] No. 67, p. 66.

[9] For a detailed discussion of the instrumental (?) nature of the *Odhecaton,* see Gustave Reese, "The First Printed Collection of Part Music: The Odhecaton," *Mus. Quart.,* XX, 1 (Jan., 1934), 62, 63.

[10] Milano, Bibl. Trivulz., MS 55, fol. 56'–57; Firenze, Bibl. Naz., MS Panc. 27, fol. 21'. The text is no. XLIV of the *Rispetti Spicciolati* in A. Poliziano, *Le stanze, l'Orfeo e le*

Angiolo's *canzoni a ballo* (usually in the form of *barzellette*) and other *canzonette* are similar in mood to those he heard with relish while wandering about the countryside near Florence. Some are ingenuous hymns to love, others ironical references to Cupid and his caprices. Both types are found in tonal setting by the frottolists, as for example the *barzellette*:[11] *Che sarà della mia vita; Io non l'ho perchè non l'ho;* and *Non potrà mai dir amore,* the second of which is published in the Appendix (see No. 1) ; the *canzone a ballo, La non vuol esser più mia;*[12] and the *canzone, Questo mostrarsi adirata di fore,* the last having been harmonized by both Heinrich Isaac and Bartholomaeus the Florentine organist.[13]

To Luigi Pulci, the third great name in the Medicean circle, are ascribed a considerable number of ardent *rispetti* or *strambotti,* several of which are retained for us in musical setting. Doubts have been expressed concerning Luigi's authorship of these plebeian verses, for many were attributed also to younger strambottists, including Serafino and Calmeta. Unassailable is the fact that the rhymes were sung throughout Italy during the last decades of Pulci's life, but it is difficult to determine whether he was the actual author or merely the collector of *poesie del popolo* which were claimed also by his rivals.

Musical examples of these, perhaps improvised by Luigi for the amusement of his beloved Lorenzo, include: *Se l'affanato core in focho iace,* set by the Venetian organist Franciscus Ana in Petrucci's *Lib. IV,* no. 36 ;[14] the ironically lugubrious *Voi che passate qui, fermate el passo!* with music by Tromboncino in Petrucci's *Lib. VII,* fol. 19 ;[15] and an eloquently exaggerated version of that popular theme, the plea for forgiveness :

Doglia mia acerba, e voi, sospiri ardenti,
Andate a quella che prigion mi serra,
Con versi lachrymosi e dolci accenti
Gridando : pace ormai di tanta guerra!

E se pur vuol ch e' miei lunghi tormenti
Chiudan la carne stanca in poca terra,
Nella sua bianca man gettati el core
Ch'assai felice è morte con honore![16]

---

rime, ed. G. Carducci (Roma, Milano, 1910), but is attributed also to Serafino in Giunta's ed. of his rhymes (Firenze, 1516), no. 406.

[11] Poliziano, *op. cit.,* pp. 251, 252, 173. Anonymous music to the first in London, Brit. Mus., MS Egerton 3051, fol. 30'–32; Marco Cara's setting of the second in Petrucci's *Lib. VII,* fol. 40', and in *Canzoni nove,* no. 29; the Venetian Joannes Lulinus' harmonization of the third in Petrucci's *Lib. XI,* 58, see Einstein, "Das elfte Buch der Frottole," *Zeitschrift f. Musikwissenschaft,* X (1927–1928), 623.

[12] Poliziano, *op. cit.,* p. 254. Tromboncino's setting in *Lib. XI,* no. 8; and in Antico's *Frottole intabulate da sonar organi* (see p. 3 n. above) ; Jac. Fogliano's in Vogel, 1515[1].

[13] Poliziano, *op. cit.,* p. 179. Isaac's music in the *D.T.Ö.,* XIV, 1, 42; Bartholomaeus' setting published by Gandolfi, *op. cit.,* pp. 537 ff., appendix p. 3.

[14] Schwartz, Pub. ält. Mus., VIII, 68; and Vogel, 1509[1], fol. 46. The third line in Schwartz's version, p. xl, should be "Se in mar turbato sto senza pace," not "pare." The text in Luigi Pulci, *Strambotti,* a cura di A. Zenatti (Firenze, 1887, 1894), I, no. 98.

[15] Also in Vogel, 1509[1], fol. 9, ascribed to Fr. Ana Ven. (*sic*) ; and in Brit. Mus., MS Egerton 3051, no. 18, see Jeppesen, "Ueber einige unbekannte Frottolenhandschriften," *Acta Mus.,* XI, 82. The text in Pulci, *op. cit.,* I, no. 27; but ascribed to Serafino in Soncino's edition of his rhymes (Fano, 1505) ; in Cod. Magl. II.II.75, see Mazzatinti, *Inventarii ... Italia,* VIII, 190; among the *strambotti* attributed "for the most part" to Serafino in Paris, Bibl. Nat., Cod. Ital. 1543, see Mazzatinti, *Inventario ... Francia,* II, 537; but ascribed also to Vincentii (Calmeta) in Cod. Vat. Urb. 729, no. 128, see Zannoni, "Strambotti inedite del sec. XV," *Rend. dell' Accad. dei Lincei,* Ser. V, I (1892), 382.

[16] Music by Al. Mantovano in Antico's *Frottole, libro tertio* (1517), see A. Einstein's ed. of the reprint (1518), *Canzoni, sonetti, strambotti et frottole, libro tertio,* Smith College Music Archives, IV (Northampton, Mass., 1941), 24. The text in Pulci, *op. cit.,* I, no. 98;

One who stood in the shadow of the great triumvirate of Florentine poets was Francesco Cei (1471–1505), a lutenist and improvisator of verses who regaled the hedonistic society of the city on the Arno with his *strambotti*. A singer who ardently praised the delights of this earth, he of course bitterly opposed Savonarola and his ideology. According to certain contemporary verses, Cei died of melancholy because he saw himself surpassed in the art of extemporary musical recitation by the famous Bernardo Accolti, "l'Unico Aretino."[17] One of Francesco's strambotti, beginning *Pietà, pietà, dolce guerriera mia,* appears in a Florentine manuscript,[18] set to music by the organist Bartholomaeus.

---

ascribed also to Serafino in Besicken's edition of his rhymes (Roma, 1503), no. 14; in Cod. Vat. 5170, no. 190, see Menghini, "Poesie inedite ... ," p. 24; and in Cod. Vat. Urb. 729, no. 187, see Zannoni, *op. cit.,* p. 384.

[17] V. Rossi, *Il quattrocento, storia letteraria d'Italia* (Milano: Vallardi, 1933), p. 563, n. 55.

[18] R. Ist. Musicale, MS B 2440, 2. The poem printed by S. Ferrari, *Biblioteca di letteratura popolare italiana,* I, 304.

V. ISABELLA AND MUSICAL TEXTS BY THE "LITERARY" POETS, CORREGGIO, TEBALDEO, BEMBO, SANNAZZARO, AND ARIOSTO

THAT ISABELLA D'ESTE enjoyed not only the polished rhymes of cultured poets, but also on occasion rhymes of simpler taste and origin, should be evident from the account of her literary relationship with Del Carretto and Serafino. She stimulated the production of all the talents in her entourage, whether their verses were of the popular order or otherwise. Most of the writers, however, who were favored by her praise or patronage were not strambottists but those who strove for classical elegance in poetry and sought to revive the forms and ideals of the golden *trecento*. Not satisfied with the mere recitation of Petrarchan or neoclassical verses which had been sent to her by the most genial literati of her time, the Marchioness often ordered that their lyrical beauty be enhanced through musical accompaniment. It is this fact which is of musicological importance, since Isabella thus, perhaps unwittingly, gave her blessing to a vital change in the quality of secular vocal music. With Tromboncino, Cara, and others at her beck and call, she was partial to the combination of aristocratic poetry with music. So devoted was she to the quest for beauty in word and tone that her name should be inscribed high in the list of those who lifted Italian song of the *cinquecento* from the level of the streets to the height of true art.

It is highly significant in this respect to know that Isabella gave not merely lip service to the cult of Petrarca, but genuinely admired his works and desired to hear them in musical setting. She apparently wrote to her literary friends asking them to name their favorites among the *canzoni* of the master, in order that Tromboncino might harmonize them and thereby increase her pleasure in hearing them recited. Proof of this exists in Isabella's correspondence with the soldier-poet Niccolò da Correggio, to whom she wrote on August 20, 1504: "Since I want to have a *canzone* of Petrarca set to music, I beg of your excellency to select one which pleases you and to send me the initium, along with one or two of your own favorite verses."[1] Correggio answered on August 23: "In respect to the *canzone* by Petrarca . . . I have selected one of those which pleases me most, beginning : *Sì è debile il filo a cui s'atiene.* It seems to me that it will adapt itself well to music, for it contains verses which gradually increase, then decrease in intensity."[2] Niccolò also enclosed a *canzone* of his own, written in imitation of *Sì è debile,* so that it could be sung to the same melody.

In Petrucci's seventh volume of *frottole* (1507), that of the earlier period which shows most clearly the trend toward classical verse schemes and nobler sentiments, there are printed three of Petrarca's *canzoni* in tonal settings by Tromboncino,[3] including (1) Correggio's choice, (2) *Che debb'io far?* and

---

[1] A. Luzio and R. Renier, "Niccolò da Correggio," *Giorn. Stor.*, XXI (1893), 247.
[2] *Ibid.*, p. 243.
[3] Fols. 4', 13', and 31', respectively. The first may be found also in *Canzoni nove*, no. 33; Vogel, 1509¹, fol. 5; and Antico's organ tablature (see p. 3 n. above) ; the second in *Canzoni*

(3) *S' i' 'l dissi mai*. All have been transcribed into modern notation for inclusion in the Appendix (Nos. 7, 8, and 9).

Sì è debile in Tromboncino's harmonization seems to have enjoyed some fame, for the "scourge of princes," Pietro Aretino, mentions the poem in a context which unmistakably identifies it with the Mantuan composer. In the prologue to his comedy, *Il Marescalco*, Aretino speaks derisively of the amorous ways affected by the Petrarchan and pseudo-Spanish dandies who filled the courts: "How well *I* could play someone assassinated by love! There is no Spaniard, no Neapolitan who could vanquish me in copiousness of sighs, in abundance of tears, and in the ceremony of my speech. I should appear completely bedecked with luxurious ornaments, with a page behind me dressed in the colors which had been presented to me by my goddess; and at every step I should have my shoes polished to the ultimate degree; and shaking my plume, I should circle about the walls of her residence, singing in a subdued voice: *Ogni loco mi attrista, ove io non veggio* [from *Sì è debile*, first line of the third strophe]. I should have madrigals written in her honor, and have Tromboncino set them to music; and in my cap I should carry an emblem containing a fishhook [*amo*], a dolphin [*delfino*] and a heart [*core*], which could be deciphered, 'I love you with all my heart!' "

Correggio, who had suggested *Sì è debile* to Isabella, was himself possessed of no mean talent. In his poetry he strove for and often achieved that lofty eloquence which characterizes Petrarca's songs in honor of Madonna Laura. Niccolò gladly complied with Isabella's frequent requests for new verses, and over a period of years sent her a large assortment of *canzoni*, sonnets, and *capitoli*, all of which afforded singular pleasure to the Marchioness.[4]

The poet's intimacy with the family d'Este was thus an indirect but important reason for the growing literary quality of musical texts utilized by Tromboncino and Cara. Evidently his influence was felt far beyond Mantua, for his sonnet *Quest'è quel locho, amore, se'l li ricorda*[5] was set to music by the organist at St. Mark's in Venice, Franciscus Ana, and was printed by Petrucci in *Lib. II*, 3. Correggio's authorship is here especially significant, for his poem is the first sonnet to appear in Petrucci's collections and thus marks a notable milestone on the way from *frottola* to madrigal. (See No. 6 of the Appendix.)

Born in Ferrara in 1463, Antonio Tebaldeo watched young Isabella d'Este grow up in the literary and artistic atmosphere of that court, and was her preceptor in the art of versifying both before and after her marriage to Frederic Gonzaga, Marquis of Mantua, in 1490.[6] Shortly after the young bride left

---

nove, no. 32; Vogel, 1509[1], fol. 8; Firenze, R. Ist. Mus., MS B 2440, p. 148; Bibl. Naz., Cod. Magl. XIX, 164–167, no. 36, see Alfred Einstein, "Dante, on the Way to the Madrigal," *Mus. Quart.*, XXV, 2 (April, 1939), 148–149; and Antico's organ tablature (see p. 3 n. above); the last-named in *Canzoni nove*, no. 6; and Vogel, 1509[1], fol. 7.

[4] Luzio and Renier, "Niccolò da Correggio," *Giorn. Stor.*, XXI, 258 ff.

[5] See the list of poems in Alda Arata, *Niccolò da Correggio nella vita letteraria e politica del tempo suo* (Bologna, 1934), p. 209; printed as sonnet no. 57 in R. Renier, *Canzioneretto adespoto di Nicc. da Correggio* (Torino, 1892).

[6] A. Luzio, *I precettori d'Isabella d'Este* (Ancona, 1887), pp. 51–52, 61–62.

Ferrara she began to write Tebaldeo,[7] eagerly requesting his newly composed verses until his entrance into Mantuan employ in 1496 made correspondence only rarely necessary. Two years later an edition of the poet's rhymes, dedicated to Isabella, was published surreptitiously by a cousin. If one is to judge from the use the Marchioness made of verses by other acquaintances, it is probable that Tebaldeo's also were often set to music by Tromboncino and Cara. Late in 1499, Antonio left Isabella's service, and subsequently became secretary to Lucrezia Borgia, Duchess of Ferrara. Nevertheless, his literary intimacy with Isabella continued for several years, if his offer (May 9, 1504) to pay the Marchioness with verses for a gift of shirts may be taken as evidence.[8]

Isabella as Tebaldeo's pupil and admirer must have been profoundly affected by his poetical tastes, those of an avowed Petrarchan. Antonio was not by predilection a writer of popular verses in which the familiar tone of plebeian love-making was predominant. In contrast to contemporary improvisators, his work consisted primarily of sonnets, *capitoli*, or *epistole*, and other lofty literary forms. These brought him the same amount of approbation from an appreciative if restricted audience of the intellectual aristocracy as that received by Serafino from a somewhat lower level of society. Isabella d'Este was a most influential member of that audience, one whose contribution to a change in musical standards has already been discussed in conjunction with the achievements of Niccolò da Correggio. In like manner, Tebaldeo's artistry was reflected in Isabella's choice of the texts which were set to music by the composers in her service and by others who were directly or indirectly linked to the Mantua-Ferrara-Urbino coterie.

One of the first sonnets to be printed in Petrucci's collections (*Lib. IV*, no. 7)[9] was penned by the Ferrarese poet, *Va, posa l'archo e la pharetra, amore.* Antonio's *capitoli, La insupportabil pena e'l focho ardente,*[10] printed also by Petrucci (*Lib. IX*, 59) in a setting by Andrea Antico, *Non expecto già mai con tal desio,*[11] and the sonnet identified by Einstein[12] in *Lib. XI, Non più saette amor,* are three more straws which show in which direction the wind of literary and musical taste was blowing. That the poet now and then lowered the bars and wrote popular verse is only natural. One such concession to prevailing taste was his ode, *Tu te lamenti a torto,* which with melody and harmony by Michele Pesenti was printed by Petrucci in his first book (no. 53).[13] This sprightly protestation of undying love was so constantly on the lips of the

---

[7] A. Luzio and R. Renier, "Coltura e relazioni letterarie d'Isabella d'Este," *Giorn. Stor.,* XXXV (1900), 194 ff.

[8] *Ibid.,* p. 206.

[9] Schwartz, Pub. ält. Mus., VIII, 50. The text in A. Tebaldeo, *Versi da un ms. della Biblioteca Communale Eugubina,* ed. O. Nardi (Perugia, 1906), p. 12; see also Mazzatinti, *Inventarii ... d'Italia,* I (Forli, 1891), 132.

[10] Tebaldeo, *op. cit.,* pp. 74 ff.; see also Mazzatinti, *Inventarii ... d'Italia,* I, 133.

[11] Firenze, Bibl. Naz., MS Panc. 27, fol. 17, and Vogel, 1515[1]. The poem is the first *epistola* in the Venetian ed. of Tebaldeo's rhymes (1500), and is attributed to him in the Cod. Est. VIII.*.20, fol. 149–151, see C. Frati, *Lettere di G. Tiraboschi al Padre I. Affò* (Modena, 1895), p. 583.

[12] "Das elfte Buch der Frottole," *Zeit. f. Musikw.,* X, 615.

[13] Also in Firenze, R. Ist. Mus., MS B 2441, without indication of its authorship. The text in Tebaldeo, *op. cit.,* p. 77; see also Mazzatinti, *Inventarii ... d'Italia,* I, 134.

populace that its melody seems to have been as familiar as that of a folk song. Its popularity seems also to have found it a place in devotional singing, for according to a contemporary manuscript the laud *Salve, Vergin Regina* was chanted to the same music (*cantasi come 'Tu tti lamenti a ttorto'*).[14]

Tebaldeo too had disciples among the contemporary rhymesters, not the least of whom was Serafino himself. According to Calmeta's biography, Aquilano was so taken by the polished sonnets of the Ferrarese that he devoted all his efforts to their imitation, in what were to be the last years of his life. Another whose verses show a marked affinity to those of the master was Jacopo Corsi, who expressed his admiration for Antonio in a well-turned sonnet.[15] Corsi, called by Paolo Cortese[16] an exceptionally fine improvisator, sang his own verse, accompanying himself on the lyra (a stringed instrument played with a bow). He chose to obtain his living by entertaining princes and *condottieri* at their courts, and soon gained the patronage of Roberto Sanseverino. In 1487 when Sanseverino, a general of the Venetian army, died, Jacopo sought another protector, finding him in the person of the Duke of Milan. The exact circumstances of the poet's death are not known; it is certain only that he was assassinated in one of the last years of the fifteenth century.[17] One of his elegant *capitoli*, entitled *Li angelici (onorati) sembianti e la beltade* was printed by Petrucci (*Lib. IV*, no. 10)[18] in close proximity to the Tebaldean sonnet, *Va, posa l'archo* (see p. 26 above).

Tebaldeo's friend, Pietro Bembo (1470–1547), did much to legitimize the Tuscan vulgar tongue as the literary language of Italy, but only because he himself was such a master of Latin and Greek was his attitude approved by the other Humanists. A Petrarchan to the ultimate degree, Bembo's placidly melancholy poetry is noted more for its formal lucidity than for its originality. In one respect, however, that of literary correctness, it set the standard for all subsequent generations of *cinquecento* poets.

The cult of Petrarca, so fateful in its effect on musical poetry, was enormously stimulated by Aldo Manuzio's publication of the master's *Canzoniere* in 1501, the edition having been prepared by Bembo. Bembo's first sustained Petrarchisms were *Gli Asolani*, prose dialogues with poetical insertions which glorified love and were dedicated to Lucrezia Borgia, whom Bembo had successfully courted while at Ferrara. Although *Gli Asolani* were written between the years 1498 and 1502, they were not published until 1505. Shortly after this date, one of the madrigalesque *canzonette* contained therein, *Non si vedrà*

---

[14] Firenze, Bibl. Naz., MS Palat. 169 (515), no. 10; see Italy, Ministero della Pubblica Istruzione, *Indicii e Cataloghi*, IV, *I Codici Palatini* (Roma, 1889), 156.

[15] F. Flamini, "Jacopo Corso e il Tebaldeo," *Giorn. Stor.*, XVII (1891), 396.

[16] V. Rossi, "Di una rimatrice e di un rimatore del sec. XV. Girolama Corsi Ramos e Jacopo Corsi," *Giorn. Stor.*, XV (1890), 200.

[17] G. Rossi, "Il Codice Estense X.*.34," *Giorn. Stor.*, XXX (1897), 21, n. 50.

[18] Schwartz, Pub. ält. Mus., VIII, 51, where the phrase beginning "*A date*" should be corrected to "*A darte*," according to Corsi's text, which may be found printed among the verses erroneously attributed to Serafino in Menghini, *Le rime di Serafino* ... (Bologna, 1894), pp. 325 ff. See also V. Rossi, "Di una rimatrice ... " *Giorn. Stor.*, XV, 214.

giamai stanca nè satia[19] was set to music by the Brescian Antonius Capriolus and printed in Petrucci's *Lib. VII,* from which it has been transcribed for inclusion (No. 10) in the Appendix of this monograph.

Non si vedrà affords the earliest proof of Bembo's appeal to the frottolists. It was of course an isolated example of neoclassical poetry, no more indicative of the trend toward the madrigal than any other, yet it marks the beginning of the future Cardinal's influence. This was to grow more and more noticeable during the second and third decades of the century, when other *canzoni* from *Gli Asolani,* as well as some of Bembo's miscellaneous rhymes, were found suitable for harmonization.

As far as may be determined from the index of *capoversi* to Petrucci's *Lib. XI,*[20] the piece beginning *Voi mi ponesti in foco*[21] is a *canzone* from Bembo's prose dialogues, in musical setting by Eustachius Gallus. Two others, also from *Gli Asolani,* are positively identifiable in a musical manuscript written about 1520:[22]

> *Amor, la tua virtute*
> *Non è dal mondo et da la gente intesa; ...*

and

> *Quand'io penso al martyre,*
> *Amor, che tu mi dai gravoso et forte, ...*

Although Bembo and Isabella d'Este did not actually meet before 1505, the two had corresponded earlier, and the poet had sent his admirer several newly composed verses.[23] In 1501, Isabella wrote to Lorenzo da Pavia requesting a copy of Petrarca's *Canzoniere* in Bembo's edition, publication of which was imminent. In Lorenzo's reply, Bembo is mentioned as *aficionatissimo a la S.V.,*[24] which probably refers to a literary friendship based on their mutual adherence to the Petrarchan cult. It is also known that a beautiful copy of *Gli Asolani,* printed on parchment, formed part of Isabella's library.[25]

When Bembo, through Tebaldeo's good offices, finally went to Mantua in June, 1505, to meet Isabella, he received an extremely cordial welcome. We are told that both Gonzagas were impressed by the poet's personality and talents, and that during one evening of his all-too-brief sojourn Isabella herself sang verses *by other poets,* accompanying herself with music written probably by Tromboncino or Cara. The experience must have been delightful, for shortly after his return to Venice Bembo sent the Marchioness sonnets and *strambotti* of his own composition, in the hope that she might recite and sing

[19] Cardinale Pietro Bembo, *Opere,* I: *Gli Asolani,* Lib. II (Milano: Classici Italiani, 1808), 108–109.
[20] Einstein, "Das elfte Buch der Frottole," *Zeit. f. Musikw.,* X, 623.
[21] Bembo, *op. cit.,* I, 43.
[22] Bibl. Marciana, MSS Ital. Cl. IV, No. 1795–1798, nos. 49 and 38, respectively; see Jeppesen, *Acta Mus.,* XI, 96. The texts in Bembo, *op. cit.,* I, 10, 39.
[23] V. Cian, "Pietro Bembo e Isabella d'Este Gonzaga," *Giorn. Stor.,* IX (1887), 95.
[24] Luzio and Renier, "Coltura ... Isabella d'Este," *Giorn. Stor.,* XXXIII (1899), 17.
[25] *Ibid.,* XXXVII (1901), 204.

his verses also, as sweetly and suavely as she had performed the others on that happy evening.[26]

These rhymes and those which subsequently found their way to the Mantuan court were in all probability harmonized by Isabella's composers, but to my knowledge only one such setting has been preserved, Tromboncino's version of the *canzone:*

> Gioia m'abonda al cor tanta e sì pura,
> Tosto che la mia donna scorgo et miro,
> Che 'n un momento, ad ogni aspro martiro
> In ch'ei giacesse, lo ritoglie et fura.[27]

The fact that Bembo, who in 1530 so conscientiously emulated Petrarca that he omitted all plebeian verse from his *Canzoniere,* should at this time still have been writing *strambotti* for the gratification of his feminine friends, is most revealing. At a later point in his literary career, Bembo renounced all forms which he considered insufficiently elegant, such as the *strambotto* and the *barzelletta,* and decided to confine his future poetical efforts to the noble types which had flourished during the epoch of Petrarca. By ignoring the popular patterns, he hoped to assist in eradicating them from artistic Italian poetry.

The effect of this policy on the music of subsequent decades must have been a salutary one, but from the circumstances mentioned above it is obvious that Bembo was not of one mind regarding poetical standards during the first decade of the sixteenth century, the years which mark an initial change in the quality of musical texts. It should be recognized that the Cardinal-to-be contributed to the transformation, but he alone did not cause it to come about; others were equally responsible: Correggio, Tebaldeo, and especially the magnet to whom they all were drawn, Isabella.

A poet of similar distinction, Jacopo Sannazzaro, was at Blois during February, 1503, sharing the exile of his king, Frederic of Aragon, when Isabella, through an emissary at the French court, begged to be allowed to read some of his newly written sonnets.[28] Her correspondence shows that she maintained a constant interest in Sannazzaro's work during the years which followed. In May, 1515, the Marchioness sent several *frottole* and *canzoni* by Marco Cara to a friend, the Marchese di Bitonto, asking in exchange a certain *capitolo* of Sannazzaro.[29] Bitonto answered thanking her for the music, but expressing his keen disappointment that a favorite piece beginning *"Cantai ... "* had been omitted. This referred, no doubt, to Cara's setting of Baldassare Castiglione's *Cantai, mentre nel cor lieto fioria* (see p. 34). In December of the same year, Sannazzaro's *capitolo* was dispatched to Mantua with Bitonto's accompanying remark, "It would please me greatly to hear you sing it to the accompaniment

---

[26] V. Cian, *op. cit.,* p. 102.
[27] Petrucci, *Lib. XI,* 66; and Bibl. Marciana, MSS Ital. Cl. IV, No. 1795–1798, no. 44; see Jeppesen, "Ueber einige unbekannte Frottolenhandschriften," *Acta Mus.,* XI, 96, where the *capoverso* is printed incorrectly as "Gloria m'abonda." Text in Bembo, *op. cit.,* II, 53.
[28] Luzio and Renier, "Coltura ... d'Isabella d'Este," *Giorn. Stor.,* XL (1902), 306.
[29] *Ibid.,* pp. 310–311.

of your viola." Although very little of the music which Isabella sang to Sannazzaro's poems has been preserved, it is probable that the *capitolo* referred to was that harmonized by Tromboncino, beginning:

> *Dura passion, che per amor sopporto,*
> *Veggio di nuove spoglie il mondo adorno;*
> *E non veggio il bel volto che m'ha morto,*
> *E il sol più vago a rimenar il giorno.*[30]

In addition, two of the poet's *canzoni* exist in musical setting by the Mantuan frottolists: one of them is Cara's version of

Perchè piangi, alma, se dal pianto mai	*Tanta letizia della speme harei,*
Fin non speri a toi guai?	*Che pianger non potrei.*
Per questo sol piang'io,	*Però for di speranza*
Che se agli affanni mei	*Lagrimar sol m'avanza.*[31]
Promettesse riposo al pianto mio,	

And the other is Tromboncino's of *Se per colpo del vostro altiero (fiero) sdegno.*[32]

Jacopo's verses seem to have appealed but little to the other frottolists before 1510, when his *canzone, Valle riposte e sole, Deserte piagge,*[33] was printed in the *Canzoni nove,* 31, in a musical setting by Francesco Fogliano. Some ten years later, Sannazzaro's poem in the form of a Petrarchan madrigal:[34]

Quando vostri begli occhi un caro velo	*Trascorre, sì ch'a poco io manco,*
Ombrando copre, simplicetto et bianco,	*Et l'alma per diletto si consuma:*
D'una gelata fiamma il cor s'alluma,	*Così morendo vivo, et con quell'armi*
Madonna, et le medole un caldo gielo	*Che m'occidete, voi potete aiutarmi*

was included in a manuscript collection of music now in the St. Mark's library,[35] but the composer has remained anonymous.

Isabella was familiar with Lodovico Ariosto's epic poem *Orlando Furioso* as early as the year 1507, when the great man paid a visit to Mantua, spending the better part of two days in the narration of his work.[36] The Marchioness kept herself informed of its subsequent progress and listened with rapt attention to excerpts read by the author on visits to Ferrara. Her attitude no doubt stimulated Ariosto to speed completion of the poem, which was published in

---

[30] Jacopo Sannazzaro, *Le opere volgari* (Padova, 1723), p. 434 (copy in the library of the University of Illinois). The music in *Frottole de M. Bort. Tromboncino e de M. M. Cara ... per cantar et sonar col lauto* (n.d.), fol. 16 (*tavola* only of the copy in the R. Ist. Musicale, Firenze); also in Bibl. Marciana, MSS Ital. Cl. IV, No. 1795–1798, no. 18; and in Vogel, 1519[1], 1520[1].

[31] Sannazzaro, *op. cit.,* p. 435. The music in the Bibl. Marciana, MSS Ital. Cl. IV, No. 1795–1798, no. 77; see Jeppesen, *Acta Mus.,* XI, 99, for further sources.

[32] Sannazzaro, *op. cit.,* p. 371. The music in Petrucci, *Lib. XI,* no. 6, and in Firenze, R. Ist. Mus., MS B 2495.

[33] Sannazzaro, *op. cit.,* p. 372; also Tonelli, *L'amore nella poesia ...* , p. 58.

[34] The poetical form of the *trecento* madrigal is more regular than that of its sixteenth-century namesake. In this instance, three-line strophes rhyming *abc, abc* are followed by an epigram, *dd;* differing somewhat from this pattern is the madrigal printed in the Appendix, No. 11, the lines of which rhyme *aba, cbc,* (epigram) *dede.* All lines are endecasyllabic and are generally in iambic meter.

[35] Cod. Ital. Cl. IV, No. 1795–1798, no. 35. The text in Sannazzaro, *op. cit.,* p. 356.

[36] R. Renier, "Spigolature Ariosteche," *Giorn. Stor.,* XX (1892), 304.

Ferrara, April 22, 1516. In May of the same year Lodovico went personally to Mantua to present copies of his masterpiece to the Marquis and to Isabella.

One of the most lyrical stanzas from *Orlando,* beginning *Queste non son più lachrime* (Canto 23, no. 126), was set to music by Tromboncino,[37] but it is difficult to determine whether he did so at the instance of Isabella while still in Mantuan service (before 1513), or because he knew Ariosto personally in Ferrara. I am inclined to favor the former hypothesis. It is of musicological interest that Tromboncino here unwittingly revived a medieval form, the *chanson de geste,* although in so doing he chose one of the least epic of Ariosto's stanzas.

---

[37] *Frottole de M. Bort. Tromboncino ...* , fol. 45–45′; Bibl. Marciana, MSS Ital. Cl. IV, No. 1795–1798, no. 67; Vogel, 1520¹, fol. 3′–4. See Albino Zenatti, *Una stanza del Furioso musicata da Bart. Tromboncino* (Firenze, 1889). It was impossible to find this pamphlet in American libraries, but its title alone served as the point of departure for a successful investigation by the author.

VI. THE INSERTION OF FROTTOLE INTO DRAMATIC REPRESENTATIONS

MUSICAL *barzellette* and other canzonets were regularly introduced into the plays in vogue during the epoch of the *frottola,* some as intermezzi between the acts, some as motivated soliloquies or even choral commentaries sung during the course of the action. For example, it has been shown[1] that a number of lyrical verses in Poliziano's mythological fable *Orfeo,* produced at the Mantuan court in 1480, were chanted to music composed by a certain Germi. These included Aristeo's *canzone,* accompanied by Mopso on his syrinx, a chorus of Driads, Orfeo's prayer to the infernal spirits, and the finale, a chorus of Bacchantes. The insertion of such music into *Orfeo* was of course but another point of resemblance to the long-established *Sacre Rappresentazioni,* which were replete with popular songs, lauds, dance music, and like forms of entertainment.

The many secular dramas, both comedies and tragedies, pastoral eclogues, and other genres of representation in which music played a sufficiently important role to warrant their consideration as precursors of the opera, have been listed and described at length by several authors.[2] Only one typical example need therefore be cited here, the manuscript of a tragedy written by Jacopo del Legname da Treviso in 1517, in which are contained detailed directions for the performance of certain sung intermezzi: At the end of Act I "a choir of four rustics, that is, two men and two women, led by Mercury" sang verse after verse of the *frottola, Viva ognun chi siegue Amore in felice et lieto stato,* each one of which had first been recited by the wing-footed god. In the same antiphonal manner the *frottola, Tuto vince el fiero amore,* was heard between the second and third acts.[3]

Such information is additional proof that *frottole* were often sung by an *a cappella* chorus, as is also the letter from Jano Pencaro to Isabella d'Este, dated February 10, 1499, in which he describes the performance of a comedy *Trinumo* with its intermezzi: "In the fourth act, five men and five ladies came forth singing a *strambotto* and then a *barzelletta,* which I shall send to your excellency together with the music."[4] From the emphasis given to a description of dancing and musical intermezzi, it may be seen that they and not the comedy itself were already the focal point of the public's interest. How clearly this portends the coming of the opera!

Musicologists have hitherto been unable to identify the music sung during such performances, since those who sang the inserted *canzonette* were more

---

[1] Pietro Canal, "Della musica in Mantova," *Memorie del R. Ist. Veneto ...,* XXI (1879), 658.

[2] A. d'Ancona, *Origini del teatro italiano* (2d ed.; Torino, 1891), 2 vols., *passim;* from which Romain Rolland obtained his information for *L'Opéra avant l'opéra* in *Musiciens d'autrefois* (10th ed.; Paris: Hachette, [n.d.]); A. Solerti, *Le origini del melodramma* (Torino, 1903); and *Gli albori del melodramma* (Milano, 1905), Vol. I; and especially Arn. Bonaventura, *Saggio storico sul teatro musicale italiano* (Livorno, 1913), pp. 1–48.

[3] V. Cian, *Le rime di B. Cavassico,* Scelta di curiosità letterarie, vv. 246, 247 (Bologna, 1893–1894), I, 246; also D'Ancona, *op. cit.,* II, 123.

[4] Luzio and Renier, "Commedie classiche in Ferrara nel 1499," *Giorn. Stor.,* XI (1888), 186.

often than not also the improvisators of the tunes. This was true of the allegorical representation written by Serafino Aquilano for performance in Mantua early in 1495. The poet himself played the part of Voluptuousness, lasciviously dressed, *"come a la Voluptà si conviene,"* singing the verses to his own accompaniment *"cum el leuto in brazo."*[5]

It has now become possible to identify several of the *frottole* written by dramatic poets intimate with Isabella d'Este, those who requested the aid of her singers Cara and Tromboncino in the composition of musical intermezzi. Galeotto del Carretto was especially prone to use both solo and choral *barzellette* in his dramatic works. One such play, an allegorical comedy called the *Nozze di Psiche e Cupidine,*[6] composed in celebration of the marriage agreement, in 1502, between Guglielmo IX (Paleologo) and Anna d'Alençon contains several examples of entr'actes, and the like, in Galeotto's favorite metrical form, one of which exists in musical setting by Tromboncino (or Cara?) :

> *Crudel, fugi se sai!*
> *Chè far tu non potrai,*
> *(Se ben patisco guai,)*
> *Chè t'habandoni mai.*
> *Crudel, fugi se sai!*[7]

Another, the music to which has apparently been lost, is that entitled, *Giove, che intende,* to be sung by a chorus after the fourth act.[8]

Early in 1499, Bartolomeo Tromboncino and other musicians were sent from Mantua to Casale to enact Carretto's comedy *Beatrice,* the text of which has unfortunately disappeared. Not only was Tromboncino a composer, singer, and instrumentalist, but an actor as well! The lyrical intermezzi to the play are known to have been harmonized by Bartolomeo,[9] but his music remains unidentifiable until such time as the play itself may again come to light.

According to a letter dated July 8, 1493,[10] an eminent member of Isabella's circle, Niccolò da Correggio, sent to Mantua a dramatic eclogue which was intended to be set to music *(uno capitolo da cantarli drento).* The text of this work, entitled *La semidea,* has been published,[11] but I was unable to identify its music, despite careful examination of a great many collections of *frottole.*

Urbino, despite its small size, has often been called the Athens of the Italian Renaissance because of the liberality of its rulers and the extraordinary concentration at its court of literati, painters, sculptors, and musicians. The Duchess Elisabeth, sister of Isabella d'Este, sang and played the lute with

---

[5] F. Torraca, *Il teatro italiano* (Firenze, 1885), p. 327.
[6] An example [n.d.] in the Bibl. Reale, Torino, see R. Reniér, "Saggio di rime inedite di Galeotto del Carretto," *Giorn. Stor.,* VI (1885), 234, n. 1.
[7] Text published by A. Saviotti, "Di un codice musicale del sec. XVI," *Giorn. Stor.,* XIV (1889), 246, n. 1. The music is ascribed to Cara in Antico's organ tablature (see p. 3 n. above), but to Tromboncino in 1518[1], see Einstein's ed. of *Canzoni, sonetti ...* , Smith College Music Archives, IV, 56. It is anonymous in the Bibl. Marciana, MSS Ital. Cl. IV, No. 1795–1798, no. 59.
[8] Renier, "Saggio di rime inedite ... ," *Giorn. Stor.,* VI, 244, n. 6.
[9] *Ibid.,* p. 236.
[10] Luzio and Renier, "Niccolò da Correggio," *Giorn. Stor.,* XXI (1893), 247.
[11] G. Rossi, "Il Codice Estense X.*.34," *Giorn. Stor.,* XXXII (1898), 102.

sufficient skill to merit the praise of all who were privileged to hear. She and her courtiers were extremely fond of music in all its forms, especially that heard in conjunction with theatrical representations. Frequent reference to these arts is made by Castiglione in his *Cortegiano,* a timeless analysis of Renaissance courtliness and culture with Urbino as its locale. In Elisabeth's circle were heard also those literary discussions which have since become classic, in which Pietro Bembo, the Cardinal Bibbiena, and Castiglione himself participated.

In 1504 Castiglione shared his lodgings in Urbino with a cousin and close friend, Cesare Gonzaga (*ca.* 1475–1512), who was later to collaborate with him in the composition of *Tirsi,*[12] a dramatic eclogue. At the carnival of 1506 the two recited this work at court, much to the delight of the Duchess Elisabeth and her intimates. Such eclogues represented idyllic scenes which have been regarded as the precursors of Tasso's pastoral drama, *Aminta.* They were performed at first with few or no stage properties and usually served as entertainment for guests at banquets and other festive occasions. Both Castiglione and Gonzaga were dressed as shepherds, and, according to custom, displayed their musical as well as their histrionic abilities. One of the *canzonette* sung by Iola (Castiglione), beginning:

> *Queste lacrime mie, questi sospiri,*
> *Son dolce cibo della mia nemica*[13]

is identifiable in a setting by Tromboncino which was included in a number of *frottola* collections.[14] This strongly suggests the possibility that Bartolomeo wrote all the music performed in the eclogue, as he had done so often for the dramatic enterprises of Carretto.

Another piece of evidence concerning the literary and musical relationship between Isabella and Castiglione is Cesare Gonzaga's letter of December 2, 1510,[15] in which he asks the Marchioness to have Cara harmonize a poem of his, and also requests her to send the air to a sonnet: *Cantai, mentre nel cor lieto fioria* (which is by Castiglione).[16] The picture becomes complete when one discovers that Cara's setting of Castiglione's sonnet was printed in Antico's organ tablatures of *frottole* (see p. 3 n. above) and in other contemporary collections.[17]

---

[12] Edited by F. Torraca, *op. cit.,* pp. 422 ff.

[13] See P. A. Serassi, *Poesie del Castiglione* (Roma, 1760), p. 17.

[14] Petrucci, *Lib. XI,* fol. 63'–64 (B. T.); *Frottole de M. Bort. Tromboncino ...* (*tavola* only), fol. 33; Bibl. Marciana, MS cited no. 39, see Jeppesen, *Acta Mus.,* XI, 96.

[15] Carlo d'Arco, "Notizie di Isabella Estense Gonzaga," *Archivio Storico Italiano,* Ser. I, II (Firenze, 1845), 113–114; see also V. Cian's edition of *Il Cortegiano del Conte Baldesar Castiglione* (Firenze, 1906), p. xxiii.

[16] Serassi, *op. cit.,* p. 41.

[17] Vogel, 1517[1], reprinted 1518, see Alfred Einstein's edition of *Canzoni, sonetti ...* , Smith College Music Archives, IV, 61.

VII. TOWARD THE MADRIGAL

THE LITERARY trend in secular music, evident from the previous analysis, grew in strength during the 1520's until classical verses of distinction and elegance became the norm. An already active and vigorous cult of Petrarca was to achieve such influence that in subsequent decades each of the master's lyrics was set to music not once but many times.

This heightened artistry of text in the *frottola* was but one of the stylistic elements necessary to make up the balanced euphony of the madrigal. Another, later in coming, was the writing of all voice parts as independent, vocally conceived, melodic lines, each created in the image of its text. Generally speaking, a distinction was no longer made between a solo voice, the musical phrasing of which corresponded to that of its poetry, and three accompanying instrumental parts, as in the *canzoni* from *Lib. VII* printed in the Appendix. There were of course several stages in the development from Tromboncino's early *canzoni* to the full-fledged madrigal; one such stage is illustrated by Sebastian Festa's setting of the Petrarchan madrigal *Perchè al viso d'amor,* which has been transcribed from the unique volume entitled *Motetti e canzone libro primo* (1521?),[1] now in the Pierpont Morgan Library, New York (see No. 11 of the Appendix). All four voices of this and other compositions of similar type are now intended to be sung, since a full text, the divisions and accentuation of which are mirrored in the music, has been supplied to each part. Yet the lower melodic lines are not particularly vocal, for they contain a large number of awkward skips in contrast to the prevalence of diatonic steps and repeated tones in the uppermost voice; rather are they reminiscent of traditional supporting parts with a definitely instrumental flavor.

It is well known that the fully formed madrigal was the creation of composers who were not Italians but Netherlanders, notably Arcadelt, Verdelot, and Willaert. The seeming paradox becomes easier to understand if one recalls that simplicity and homophony always have been native to Italian music, and that complete independence of voice parts is more characteristic of northern Europe, that is, of the Burgundian-Franco-Flemish compositional schools. Individuality of melodic lines in a polyphonic complex has always seemed foreign to the Italian nature; imitative counterpoint in cisalpine music resembles an imported plant which occasionally bears fruit but which is usually choked by a native growth, in this case by solistic writing. The polyphonic technique evident in the Florentine *caccia,* and in the works of a Palestrina or a Frescobaldi, may be likened to the scattered examples of Gothic architecture in northern Italy; both are representative of alien concepts which rarely took deep root and which were readily supplanted by the fundamental Italian styles: classical roundness in architectonic construction and monody in music.

---

[1] See my article entitled "Madrigal," in the *International Cyclopedia of Music and Musicians,* ed. Oscar Thompson (New York: Dodd, Mead, 1939), p. 1067; and A. Einstein, "A Supplement: An Old Music Print at the J. P. Morgan Library in New York," *Mus. Quart.,* XXV, 4 (Oct., 1939), 507. The madrigal is also contained in the Cod. Magl. XIX, 164–167, no. 24, see Einstein, "Dante . . . ," *Mus. Quart.,* XXV, 2 (April, 1939), 148–149.

As the *frottola-canzone* of the transitional decades progressed toward a fuller expression of the polyphonic style, those Italians who had led the march left the procession. Yet this cannot detract from the value of their contribution to the proud record of music in the motherland. Since the *frottola* and *canzone* were indigenous art forms couched in a musical language native to the Italian of the Renaissance, familiarity with them is essential to a complete understanding of that vital period in artistic history.

APPENDIX OF MUSICAL EXAMPLES

1. IO NON L'HO—(FROTTOLA)

M[ARCO] C[ARA]

(POLIZIANO)

PETRUCCI—LIB. VII (1507), F. 40'–41

Io non l'hò per-che—— non—— l'ho, Quel ch'or-

Io non l'ho perche non l'ho (*Instr.*)

Io non l'ho perche non l'ho (*Instr.*)

Io non l'ho perche non l'ho (*Instr.*)

-mai ha-ver do-vri - a; S'io l'ha-ves-se, l'ha-ve -

(1)

- ri - a, Ma l'harò quan-do l'ha - rò. Ma l'harò quan-

(1) F-F in original.

[39]

do l'ha-rò (quan - - - - do l'ha-rò. l'ha - rò quan - - - - do l'ha - rò.)

Lon - go tem - po son ——————— vi - vu - to A -
Da chi sem - - pre m'a ——————— te - nu - to In ——

Longo tempo
Longo tempo
Longo tempo

— spec - tan - do ha ver un be - ne (ha - ver un be - ne)
spe - ran - ze e an - chor mi te - ne; (e an - chor mi te - ne);

Ma tal — ben gia - - - mai — — — — non ve - ne,

Et io in - cer - te o - - - gnhor pro - mes - se Da chi di - ce e
Vo pi - gliando ad — in - te - res - se

(1)

D.C. al Fine

tel da - rò. Da— chi - di - - ce e tel da - - rò.)

(1) Brevis rest in original.

Mille volte dico mecho:
Tu l'harai, non ti curare;
Poi respondo e dico: ciecho!
Tempo perdi in domandare;
E così con tal variare
In pensier me strugo, e rodo
E per me mai non gli è modo
De haver quel che haver si pò.
        Io non l'ho perchè non l'ho . . .

Horsù donque ala bon'hora
Io l'harò, ma non so el dì,
Chè de haver non vedo anchora
Se non ciance insino a qui;
Ma si effetto havesse el sì
Che ogni giorno ho'l pagamento,
Daria fin al vechio intento
Che suspeso è tra sì e no.
        Io non l'ho perchè non l'ho . . .

Io pur penso, e non riesce
Lo importuno mio pensiero;
E'l desir tanto più cresce
Quanto men de haverlo spero,
Talchè son dal dolor fiero.
Aspettando vinto e stanco
E di fede pur non manco,
Ma l'harò quando l'harò.
        Io non l'ho perchè non l'ho . . . .

2. SE GRAN FESTA—(FROTTOLA)

(BARTOLOMEO TROMBONCINO)

(GALEOTTO DEL CARRETTO)

MILANO, TRIVULZIANA, MS. 55 F. 46'–48

(1) G is minima in manuscript; repeat sign in manuscript alto is here, despite the fact that the repeated music is subsequently written out; repeat sign in tenor of manuscript appears three measures later.

3. NON TE STIMAR—(STRAMBOTTO)

(SERAFINO AQUILANO)

MILANO, BIBL. TRIVULZ. MS 55, F. 18'–19.

Non te sti - mar, se a te cias - cun s'a - ren - - de; (se a te cias - cun s'a - - - ren - - - - de;)

Non te sti - mar, (se a te cias - cun s'a - ren - - de; se a te cias - cun s'a - ren - - - de;)

Non te sti - mar, (se a te cias - cun s'a - ren - - de; se a te cias - cun s'a - - - - ren - - - de;)

Non te sti - mar, (se a te cias - cun s'a - ren - - de; se a te cias - cun s'a - - - - ren - - - de;)

C'o - gni fa - vor al fin tem - po l'a - bas - - -

C'o - gni fa - vor al fin tem - po l'a - bas - - - -

C'o - gni fa - vor al fin tem - po l'a - bas - - -

C'o - gni fa - vor al fin tem - po l'a - bas - - -

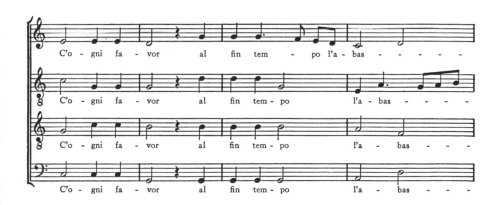

Non vedi tu che mentre el sol resplende,
L'ombra seguita l'hom, che mai lo lassa?

Ma poi, se qualche nube el ciel offende,
El sol non luze, e in quel, l'ombra passa.

Cussi te siegue ognun mentre se' in cima;
Mancato a te el favor, nullo te stima.

4. IO T'HO DONATO IL CORE—(ODE)

JOANNES BAPTISTA ZESSO

Petrucci Lib. VII (1507) f. 2

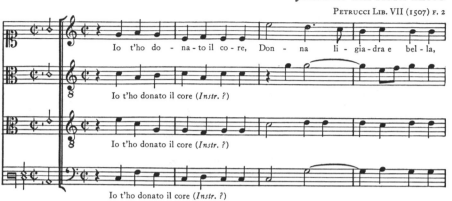

Io t'ho do - na - to il co - re, Don - na li - gia - dra e bel - la,

Io t'ho donato il core (*Instr. ?*)

Io t'ho donato il core (*Instr. ?*)

Io t'ho donato il core (*Instr. ?*)

Per - ho che tu sci quel - la ——— Che ——— tan - - - to a-

- mo ———————

Per cui ordisco e tramo
Ogni hor novo pensiero;
Per honorar tuo altiero
    E chiaro viso.

Chè con tuo dolce riso
E signoril costumi,
Mi scorzi fuor di dumi
    In fresche rose.

Non seran mai retrose
Mie voglie a compiacerte,
I' te le ho sempre offerte;
    Hora ti attendo.

Io voglio farte il mendo,
Perchè già ti fu ingrato,
Indegno e sconsolato,
    Come merta.

Sichè rimante certa,
O mia speranza viva,
Che in terra sei mia diva
    Et io tuo servo.

5. PREGOVI FRONDE, FIORI, ACQUE—(CAPITOLO)

B[ARTOLOMEO] T[ROMBONCINO]

Petrucci Lib. VII (1507), f. 11.

Pre - go-vi fronde, fio-ri, ac-que e her-be   Che al-men pres-ta - te o-

Pregovi fronde, fiori (*Instr.*)

Pregovi fronde, fiori (*Instr.*)

Pregovi fronde, fiori, (*Instr.*)

-re-chie a mie pa-ro - - le,   Men-tre ch'io sfo-co ques-te   fiamme accer - be.

(last verse only)

-to   Al sol, — al ven-to, ai tron-chi e ad o-gni sco-glio. (ai tronchi e ad o - gni — sco-glio.)

Al sol,

Al sol,

Al sol,

Rafrena il tuo bel corso, almo mio sole
E tu, fresca aura che sì dolce spiri!
Odi un che ha gran ragion d'amor si dole.

Oditi, o duri sassi, i miei suspiri,
Poi ch'altri non ascolta il mio lamento
Che fu sola cagion di miei martyri.

Io fui già tra gli amanti el più contento
Mentre fortuna e'l ciel non m'hebbe a sdegno.
Hor son il più infelice e più scontento.

Unde per non amar pongo ogni ingegno;
Ma nulla forza contra amor mi vale,
Che vince il tutto e rompe ogni disegno.

Penso el dì mille volte al mio gran male,
E fingo la mia dea cruda e defforme.
Nè pur le' extigue il fuoco aspro e mortale.

Sì arecho nel pensier mille altre forme,
E fingo hor questa, hor quella assai più bella;
Ma nulla trovo al mio martyr conforme.

Hai troppo duro fato! hai dura stella
Che me constringe amar chi me non cura,
Chi fu mai contra amor tanta ribella!

Posto ho ogni mio pensier, posto ogni cura
Sol per placar questa alma tanta altiera;
Ma sempre è più ver me spietata e dura.

Facto gli ò prova de mia fè sincera,
Et pianto ho mille volte al suo conspecto.
Nè per pianto, o per fè s'è la men fera.

Unde che in me non trovo alcun diffecto,
Poichè altro non so far, piango e mi doglio,
Narrando il grave ardor che ho dentro al pecto
Al sol, al vento, ai tronchi e ad ogni scoglio.

6. QUEST'È QUEL LOCHO, AMORE,—(SONNET)

FRANCISCUS VENE. ORGA.

(NICCOLÒ DA CORREGGIO)

Petrucci. Lib. II (1504), f. 3

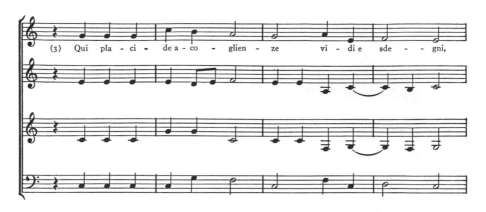

(3) Qui pla - ci - de a - co - glien - ze vi - di e sde - - gni,

Qui già fu lie - to e tal - hor se - mi mor - to,

Chè a tua for - za non val in - si - die o ingan - - - ni.

(2) Et qui la voglia, al suo mal troppo ingorda,
    Si levò al volo non havendo l'ali;
    Qui cade, chè i pensier son tutti frali
    Se'l poter col voler ben non s'accorda.

(4) Ma del color ch'io provo ho un sol conforto:
    Ch'io t'ho già rotto mille bei disegni,
    Ch'ognun al mio fallir s'è facto acorto.

7. SÌ È DEBILE IL FILO—(CANZONE)

B[ARTOLOMEO] T[ROMBONCINO]

(PETRARCA)

PETRUCCI, LIB. VII (1507), F. 4′–5′.

Sì è de - bi - le il fi - - lo a cui se at-te - ne La

Sì è debile il filo (*Instr.*)

Sì è debile il filo (*Instr.*)

Sì è debile il filo (*Instr.*)

gra-vo - sa mia vi - ta, Che, se altri non la a - i - ta, El - la fia tosto di suo corso a

ri - - - va: Pe - rò che do - po la em-pia di - par-ti - - ta Che

dal dol-ce mio be - ne Fe - ci, sol u - na spe-me E sta-to in fin a qui cagion ch'io

vi - - va, Di-cen-do: Perchè——pri-va Sia de la a-ma-ta vis-ta, Man-

- tien-te, a - ni - ma tris-ta! Che sai se a mi-glior tempo an-cho ri - tor - - - ni, Et

a più lie-ti gior-ni? O se el per-du-to ben — mai — si rac - - quis-ta? Ques-

-ta spe-ran-za mi sos-te - - - ne un tem-po; Hor vien mancan-do e trop -

-po in lei me a-tem-po. (Hor vien man-can-do e trop- - - po in lei me a-tem - po.)

Il tempo passa, e l'hore son sì pronte
A fornir il viaggio
Che assai spatio non haggio,
Pur a pensar come io corro a la morte.
A pena spunte in oriente un raggio
Di sol, che a l'altro monte
Del' adverso orizonte
Giunto el vedrai per vie lunghe e distorte.
Le vite son sì corte,
Sì gravi i corpi e frali
Degli huomini mortali,
Che quando io mi ritrovo dal bel viso
Cotanto esser diviso,
Col desio non possendo mover le ali,
Poco mi avanza del conforto usato
Nè so quanto io mi viva in questo stato.

8. CHE DEBB'IO FAR?—(CANZONE)

B[ARTOLOMEO] T[ROMBONCINO]

Petrucci Lib. VII (1507) f. 13'–14

(PETRARCA)

Che deb-b'io far? Che mi con-si-gli, a-mo - - - -
ha se-co il mio co - - - -

Che debb'io far? Che mi consigli, amore? (*Instr.*)

Che debb'io far? Che mi consigli, amore? (*Instr.*)

Che debb'io far? Che mi consigli, amore? (*Instr.*)

- re? Tem-po è ben di mo-ri-re; Et ho tar-da-to più ch'io non vor-re - -
- re; Et, vo-len-do'l se-gui-re In-ter-rom-per con-ven quest'an - ni re - -

- i. Ma-don-na è mor-ta, ed
- i; Per-chè mai ve-der lei Di qua non spe-ro, e

l'as-pec - tar m'è noi - - - a. (e l'as - pec - tar m'è noi - a.)   Pos - cia ch'ogni mia

gioi - - - - - a,   Per lo suo di-par-ti - re, —— in pian-to è

vol-ta,   E o - gni dol - cez - - za de —— mi - - - a vi-ta è tol - ta.

Amor, tu 'l senti, ond'io teco mi doglio,
Quant' è 'l danno aspro e grave;
Et so che del mio mal ti pesa e dole:
Anzi del nostro; perch' ad uno scoglio
Haven rotto la nave
Et un in punto ne è scurato il sole.
Qual ingegno a parole
Poria aguagliare il mio doglioso stato?
Ai orbo mondo ingrato!
Gran cagion hai de dover pianger meco;
Chè quel bel ch' era in te, perduto hai seco.

9. S'I' 'L DISSI MAI—(CANZONE)

B[ARTOLOMEO] T[ROMBONCINO]

Petrucci Lib. VII (1507), f. 31′–2.

(PETRARCA)

S'i' 'l dis-si mai, ch'i' ven - ga in o - dio a quel - la,   Del

S'i' 'l dissi mai, ch'i' venga in odio a quella (*Instr.*)

S'i' 'l dissi mai, ch'i' venga in odio a quella (*Instr.*)

S'i' 'l dissi mai, ch'i' venga in odio a quella (*Instr.*)

cui a - mor vi - vo e sen-za'l qual mor - - rei: S'i' 'l
dis - si ch'i miei dì sian po - chi —— e   rei,   E

di vil si - gno - rie l'a - ni - ma an-cel - - - - - la   S'i' 'l dis - si, con - tra

me s'ar — mi o-gni stel — la, E dal mio la - to si — — — a Pa-u-ra

— — e ge-lo-si — a, E la i-ni - mi - ca — mi — — —

— — a Più fe - ro - ce ver me sem — pre e più bel — — — — la.

S' i' 'l dissi, Amor l'aurate sue quadrelle
Spenda in me tutte e l'impiombate in lei:
S' i' 'l dissi, cielo e terra, huomini e Dei
Me sian contrari, ed essa ognior più fella:
S' i' 'l dissi, che con sua cieca facella
Dritto a morte m'invia,
Pur come glie è si sia,
Nè mai più dolce o pia
Ver me si mostri in atto od in favella.

S' i' 'l dissi mai, di quel che men vorrei
Piena trovi quest'aspra e breve via:
S' i' 'l dissi, il fiero ardor che mi disvia
Cresca in me, quanto el fier ghiaccio in costei:
S' i' 'l dissi, unqua non veggian li occhi mei
Sol chiaro o sua sorella,
Nè donna nè donzella,
Ma terribil procella
Qual Faraone in perseguir gli Hebrei.

10. NON SI VEDRÀ GIAMAI—(CANZONE)

A[NTONIUS] C[APRIOLUS]

(PIETRO BEMBO)

Petrucci Lib. VII (1507) f. 8'–9.

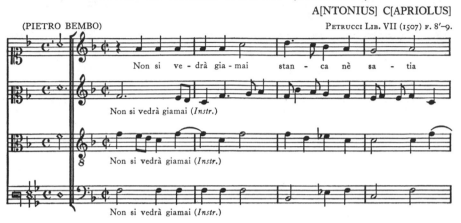

Non si ve - drà gia - mai   stan - ca nè sa - tia

Non si vedrà giamai (*Instr.*)

Non si vedrà giamai (*Instr.*)

Non si vedrà giamai (*Instr.*)

Ques - ta mia pe-na, a-mo-re,   Di ren-der - ti, si - gno-re,   Del tuo con -tan-to honor

al - cu - na gra - tia: A cui pen-san-do vo - lon-tier si spa - tia

Per la me - mo-ria il co - re; Ve - den-do il tuo va - lo - re: On - de pren-

de vi - go - re, e te rin - gra - tia———————— (On - de pren-de vi -

- go - re, e te rin - gra - - - - - tia ———————————.)

Amor, da te conosco quel ch'io sono.
Tu primo mi levasti
Da terra, e in cielo alzasti;
Et al mio dir donasti un dolce suono:
Et tu colei, di ch'io sempre ragiono,
Agli ochi miei mostrasti;
Et dentro al cor mandasti
Pensier ligiadri e casti, altero dono.

Tu sei, la tua mercè, cagion che io viva
In dolce fuoco ardendo;
Dal qual ogni ben prendo,
Di speme il cor pascendo honesta e viva:
Et se giamai verrà, che i' gionga e ariva
Là ove il mio volo extendo,
Quanto piacer ne attendo,
A pena ch'io no 'l comprendo, non ch'io il scriva.

Vita suave e cara,
Chi da te non la impara, amor, non have.

11. PERCHÈ AL VISO D'AMOR—(MADRIGAL)

SEBASTIAN FESTA

(PETRARCA)

Motetti e Canzone. Lib. Primo (1521?) No. 19

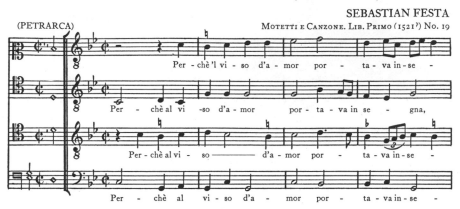

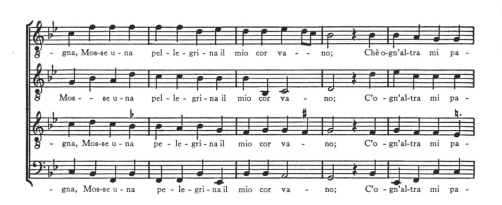

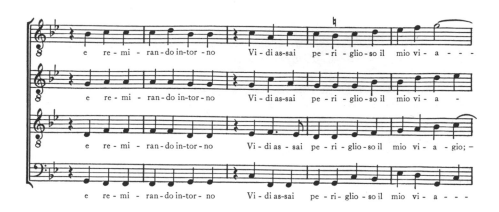

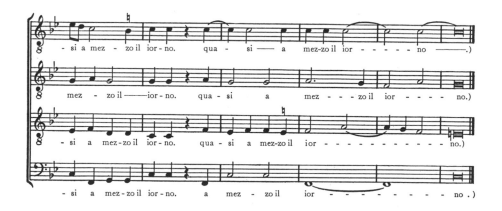

BIBLIOGRAPHY

BIBLIOGRAPHY

Literature Referring Wholly or in Part to the Musical Frottola and Its Authors

ARATA, ALDA
  Niccolò da Correggio nella vita letteraria e politica del tempo suo (Bologna: Zanichelli, 1934).

Associazione dei Musicologi Italiani. *Bollettino.*
  "Catalogo delle opere musicali ... esistenti ... nelle biblioteche e negli archivi pubblici e privati d'Italia" (Parma: Fresching, 1909 ff.).

BERTOLOTTI, ANTONINO
  Musici alla corte dei Gonzaga in Mantova dal sec. XIV al sec. XVIII (Milano, 1890).

BESSELER, HEINRICH
  Die Musik des Mittelalters und der Renaissance. Handbuch der Musikwissenschaft, her. von E. Bücken (Potsdam: Athenaion, 1931).

CANAL, PIETRO
  "Della musica in Mantova," *Memorie del R. Istituto Veneto di Scienze, Lettere ed Arti,* XXI (1879), 655 ff.

CAPPELLI, ANTONIO
  Poesie musicali dei secoli XIV, XV e XVI. Scelta di curiosità letterarie, Vol. 94 (Bologna, 1868).

CASTIGLIONE, BALDASSARE
  The Book of the Courtier, trans. by L. E. Opdyke (New York, 1903).

CESARI, GAETANO
  Die Entstehung des Madrigals im 16. Jahrhundert (Cremona, 1909). Dissertation, University of Munich.
  "Le origini del madrigale musicale cinquecentesco," *Rivista Musicale Italiana,* XIX (1912), 1–34, 380–428.
  "La cappella musicale sforzesca e le forme liriche profane," in Fr. Malaguzzi-Valeri, *La corte di Lodovico il Moro* (Milano: Hoepli, 1913 ff.), Vol. 4 (1923).
  "Musica e musicisti alla corte sforzesca," *Riv. Mus. Italiana,* XXIX (1922), 1 ff.
  Istituzioni e monumenti dell'arte musicale in Italia (Milano: Ricordi, 1932), Vol. II, Preface.

CIAN, VITTORIO
  "Pietro Bembo e Isabella d'Este Gonzaga," *Giornale Storico della Letteratura Italiana,* IX (1887), 81 ff.

D'ALESSI, GIOVANNI
  "Zanìn Bisàn (1473?–1554)," *Note d'Archivio per la Storia della Musica,* VIII (Jan., 1931), 21 ff.

D'ANCONA, ALESSANDRO
  "Il teatro mantovano nel secolo XVI," *Giorn. Stor.,* V (1885), 1 ff.
  Origini del teatro italiano (2d ed.; Torino, 1891), 2 vols.

DAVARI, STEFANO
  "La musica a Mantova," *Rivista Storica Mantovana,* I (1885), 53 ff.

EINSTEIN, ALFRED
  "Die mehrstimmige weltliche Musik von 1450–1600," *Handbuch der Musikgeschichte,* ed. Guido Adler (2d ed.; Berlin: H. Keller, 1930), Vol. I.
  "Das elfte Buch der Frottole," *Zeitschrift für Musikwissenschaft,* X (1927–1928), 613 ff.
  "Dante, on the Way to the Madrigal," *Musical Quarterly,* XXV (1939), 142 ff.
  "Italian Madrigal Verse, 1500–1600," *Proceedings of the Mus. Assoc.,* 63 (1936–1937), 79 ff.

EINSTEIN, ALFRED (*Continued*)
"A Supplement: An Old Music Print at the J. P. Morgan Library in New York," *Mus. Quart.*, XXV(1939), 507 ff.

Canzoni, sonetti, strambotti et frottole, libro tertio, Smith College Music Archives, Vol. IV (Northampton, Mass., 1941).

FERAND, ERNST T.
"Two Unknown *Frottole,*" *Mus. Quart.*, XXVII (1941), 319 ff.

FLAMINI, FRANCESCO
"Francesco Galeota ... e il suo inedito canzoniere," *Giorn. Stor.*, XX (1892), 1 ff.

GANDOLFI, RICCARDO
"Intorno al cod. membr. del R. Istituto Musicale di Firenze No. 2440," *Riv. Mus. Italiana,* XVIII (1911), 537 ff.

GASPERINI, GUIDO
"La Musique italienne au XVᵉ siècle," *Encyclopédie de la musique,* ed. Lavignac, Vol. Iª (Paris: Delagrave, 1931), 620 ff.

GHISI, FEDERICO
I canti carnascialeschi nelle fonti musicali del XV e XVI secolo (Firenze-Roma: Olschki, 1937).

"Carnival Songs and the Origins of the Intermezzo Giocoso," *Mus. Quart.*, XXV (1939), 325 ff.

Feste musicali della Firenze Medicea (1480–1589), a cura di F. Ghisi (Firenze: Vallecchi, 1939).

GOTTI, AURELIO
Vita di Michelangelo Buonarotti (Firenze, 1876), Vol. II.

GRAVISI, ANTEO
"Andrea Antico da Montona," *Atti e Memorie della Società Istriana di Archeologia e Storia Patria,* I, fasc. 1–2 (Parenzo, 1885), 141 ff.

HELM, EVERETT B.
"Heralds of the Italian Madrigal," *Mus. Quart.*, XXVII (1941), 306 ff.

I codici panciatichiani della Bibl. Naz. Centrale di Firenze (Firenze, 1887–1891), Vol. I.

JEPPESEN, KNUD
"Die neuentdeckten Bücher der Lauden des Ottaviano dei Petrucci und andere musikalische Seltenheiten der Bibl. Colombina zu Sevilla," *Zeitschrift für Musikwissenschaft,* XII (Nov. 1929), 73 ff.

"Die mehrstimmige italienische Laude am Anfang des 16. Jahrhunderts," International Society for Musical Research. *First Congress, Liège ... 1930, Report.* (Nashdom Abbey: The Plainsong and Mediaeval Society, 1931).

Die mehrstimmige italienische Laude um 1500 (Leipzig: Breitkopf u. Härtel, 1935).

"Ueber einige unbekannte Frottolenhandschriften," *Acta Musicologica,* XI, fasc. 3 (July–Sept., 1939), 81 ff.

KIWI, EDITH
Studien zur Geschichte des italienischen Liedmadrigals im 16. Jahrhundert (Würzburg: Triltsch, 1937). Dissertation, University of Heidelberg.

LAZZARI, ALFONSO
La musica alla corte dei Duchi di Ferrara (Ferrara: S. A. Industrie grafiche, 1928).

LUZIO, ALESSANDRO
Review of Bertolotti, *Musici alla corte dei Gonzaga ... ,* in the Rassegna Bibliografica, *Giorn. Stor.*, XVII (1891), 98 ff.

LUZIO, ALESSANDRO, and RENIER, RODOLFO
Mantova e Urbino: Isabella d'Este ed Elisabetta Gonzaga nelle relazioni famigliari e nelle vicende politiche (Torino, 1893).

LUZIO, ALESSANDRO, and RENIER, RODOLFO (Continued)
"Niccolò da Correggio," Giorn. Stor., XXI (1893), 205 ff.; XXII (1893), 65 ff.

"Coltura e relazioni letterarie d'Isabella d'Este," Giorn. Stor., XXXIII (1899), 1 ff.; XXXIV (1899), 1 ff.; XXXV (1900), 193 ff.; XXXVI (1900), 325 ff.; XXXVII (1901), 201 ff.; XXXVIII (1901), 41 ff.; XXXIX (1902), 193 ff.; XL (1902), 289 ff.; XLII (1903), 75 ff.

MANACORDA, GIUSEPPE
"Galeotto del Carretto. Poeta lirica," Memorie della R. Accademia delle Scienze di Torino, Ser. II, XLIX, 2 (1900), 47 ff.

MASSON, PAUL-MARIE
Chants de carnaval florentins (Paris: Senart, 1913).

PERCOPO, ERASMO
Le rime del Chariteo (Napoli, 1892), 2 vols.

PIBER, GIOVANNI. See TOMASIN, DON PIETRO

PIRRO, ANDRÉ
"Les frottole et la musique instrumentale," Revue de Musicologie, III (March, 1922), 1 ff.

RENIER, RODOLFO. See also LUZIO, ALESSANDRO
Review of Schwartz, "Die Frottole im 15. Jahrhundert," in the Rassegna Bibliografica, Giorn. Stor., IX (1887), 298 ff.

"Saggio di rime inedite di Galeotto del Carretto," Giorn. Stor., VI (1885), 231 ff.

Review of Vogel, Bibliothek der gedruckten weltlichen Vokalmusik Italiens..., in the Rassegna Bibliografica, Giorn. Stor., XXII (1893), 378 ff.

RIEMANN, HUGO
Handbuch der Musikgeschichte (2d ed.; Leipzig: Breitkopf u. Härtel, 1920), Vol. II[1].

RONDA, ACHILLE
Un poeta [Serafino] di corte della seconda metà del XV secolo (Aquila, 1923).

ROSSI, VITTORIO
"Appunti per la storia della musica," Rassegna Emiliana, I (1888), 458 ff.

Il quattrocento, storia letteraria d'Italia (Milano: Vallardi, 1933).

RUBSAMEN, WALTER H.
"Madrigal," in the International Cyclopedia of Music and Musicians, ed. Oscar Thompson (New York: Dodd, Mead, 1939).

SAVIOTTI, ALFREDO
"Di un codice musicale del secolo XVI," Giorn. Stor., XIV (1889), 234 ff.

SCHMID, ANTON
Ottaviano dei Petrucci da Fossombrone (Wien, 1845).

SCHWARTZ, RUDOLF
"Die Frottole im 15. Jahrhundert," Vierteljahrsschrift für Musikwissenschaft, II (1886), 427 ff.

"Hans Leo Hassler unter dem Einfluss der italienischen Madrigalisten," Viertelj. f. Musikw., IX (1893), 1 ff.

"Nochmals 'Die Frottole im 15. Jahrhundert,'" Jahrbuch der Musikbibliothek Peters, XXXI (1924), 47 ff.

"Zum Formenproblem der Frottole Petruccis," Theodor Kroyer Festschrift zum 60. Geburtstage (Regensburg: Bosse, 1933), 77 ff.

Ottaviano Petrucci, Frottole, Buch I und IV, Publikationen älterer Musik ... der Deutschen Gesellschaft für Musikwissenschaft, VIII (Leipzig: Breitk. u. Härtel, 1933–1935).

TOMASIN, DON PIETRO, and PIBER, GIOVANNI
Andrea Antico chierico di Montona nell' Istria, primo calcografo musicale (Trieste, 1880).

TONELLI, LUIGI
   L'Amore nella poesia e nel pensiero del Rinascimento (Firenze: Sansoni, 1933).

TORRACA, FRANCESCO
   Il teatro italiano dei secoli XIII, XIV e XV (Firenze, 1885).

TORREFRANCA, FAUSTO
   "I primordi della polifonia nel cinquecento," *Nuova Antologia di Lettere, Scienze ed Arti,* ser. 7, anno 69 (Nov. 1, 1934), pp. 107 ff.

   Il segreto del quattrocento (Milano: Hoepli, 1939).

VAN DEN BORREN, CHARLES
   "Le Madrigal," *Encyclopédie de la musique,* ed. Lavignac, Vol. II⁵ (Paris: Delagrave, 1930), 3046 ff.

VATIELLI, FRANCESCO
   "Canzonieri musicali del '500," *Riv. Mus. Italiana,* XXVIII (1921), 397–418, 617–655. (Also in *Arte e vita musicale a Bologna: studi e saggi,* Vol. I [Bologna, 1927]).

VERNARECCI, AUGUSTO
   Ottaviano de' Petrucci da Fossombrone (2d ed.; Bologna, 1882).

VOGEL, EMIL
   Bibliothek der gedruckten weltlichen Vokalmusik Italiens, 1500–1700 (Berlin, 1892). 2 vols.

WOLF, JOHANNES
   "Heinrich Isaac. Weltliche Werke," *Denkmäler der Tonkunst in Österreich,* XIV, 1 (1907).

ZENATTI, ALBINO
   "Andrea Antico da Montona," *Archivio Storico per Trieste, l'Istria e il Trentino,* I²(1881), 167 ff.

   "Nuovi appunti su A. Antico da Montona," *Arch. Stor. per Trieste, l'Istria e il Trentino,* III, 3–4 (1886), 249 ff.

   Una stanza del Furioso musicata da Bart. Tromboncino (Firenze, 1889).

OTHER GENERAL COLLECTIONS AND HISTORIES OF MUSIC WHICH CONTAIN MODERN REPRINTS OF FROTTOLE

AMBROS, AUGUST W.
   Geschichte der Musik, Vol. V, ed. O. Kade (Leipzig, 1882 ff.).

BARBIERI, FRANCISCO (ed.)
   Cancionero musical de los siglos XV y XVI (Madrid, 1890).

CHILESOTTI, O.
   Saggio sulla melodia popolare del cinquecento (Milano, 1889).

DUFFLOCQ, ENRICO MAGNI
   Storia della musica (2d ed.; Milano: Soc. Editrice Libraria, 1933), Vol. I.

EINSTEIN, ALFRED
   Beispielsammlung zur älteren Musikgeschichte (Leipzig and Berlin: B. G. Teubner, 1917 ff.)

FERAND, ERNST T.
   Die Improvisation in der Musik (Zürich: Rhein-Verlag, 1938).

KÖRTE, OSWALD
   Laute und Lautenmusik bis zur Mitte des 16. Jahrhunderts, Publikationen der Internationalen Musikgesellschaft, Beihefte. Heft 3 (Leipzig, 1901), Anhang.

NEF, KARL
   An Outline of the History of Music, trans. C. F. Pfatteicher (New York: Columbia Univ. Press, 1935).

RIEMANN, HUGO
  Musikgeschichte in Beispielen (Leipzig, 1912 ff.).

SCHERING, ARNOLD
  Geschichte der Musik in Beispielen (Leipzig: Breitkopf u. Härtel, 1931).

TORCHI, LUIGI
  L'arte musicale in Italia (Milano: Ricordi, 1897 ff.), Vol. I.

WESTPHAL, KURT (ed.)
  "Karnevalslieder der Renaissance," *Das Chorwerk*, ed. F. Blume, Heft 43 (Wolfenbüttel-Berlin: Kallmeyer, 1936).

WOLF, JOHANNES
  Sing- und Spielmusik aus älterer Zeit (Leipzig: Quelle und Meyer, 1926 ff.).

INDEX

INDEX

CAPOVERSI

PRINCIPAL PERSONS AND SUBJECTS